Gratitude to God. Gratitude to Life. Gratitude to my family and friends.

VANESSA S.I
2024

This Book Belongs to:

V.S.I.P©
vanessa s.i publications

Test Color Page

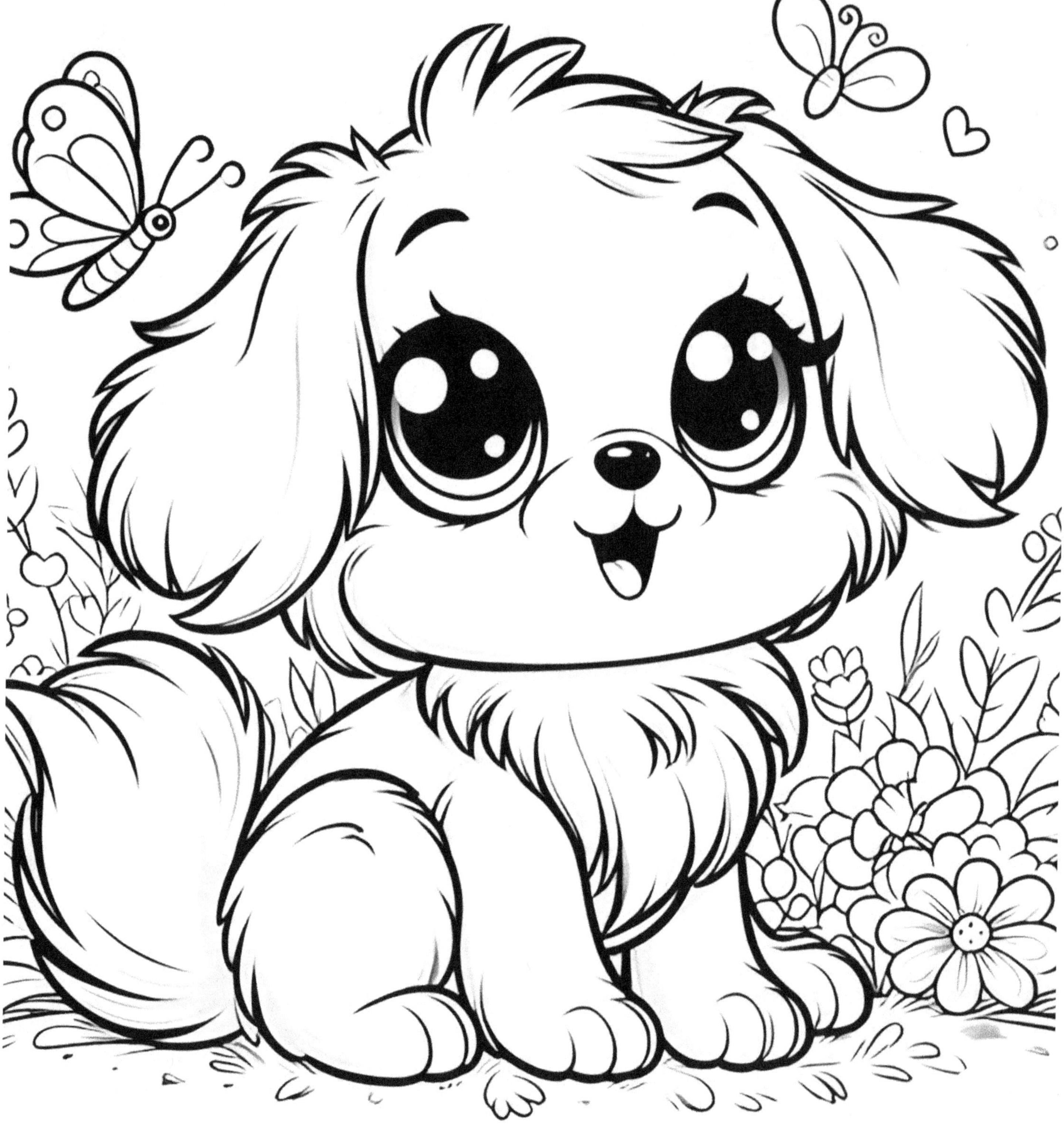

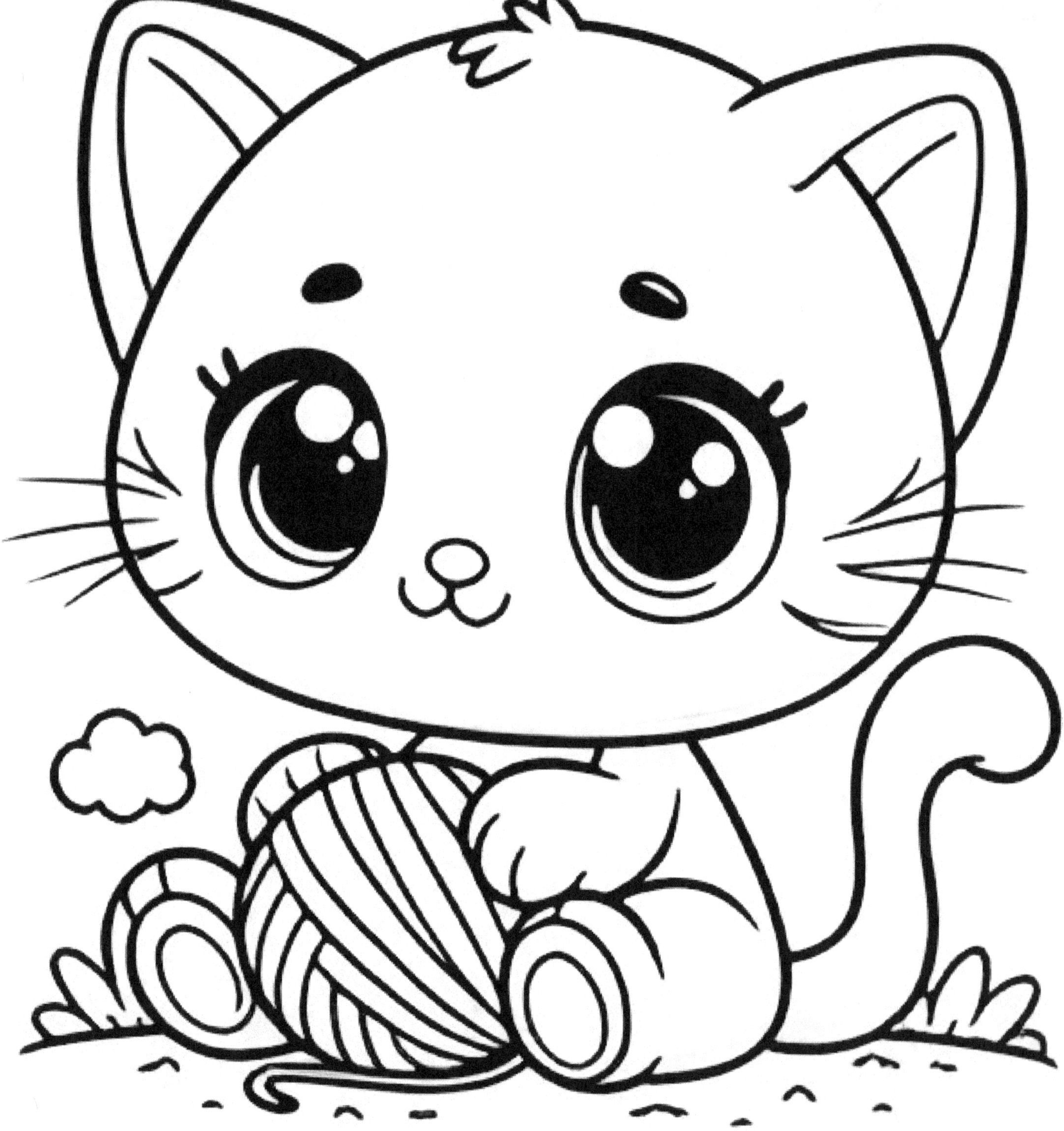

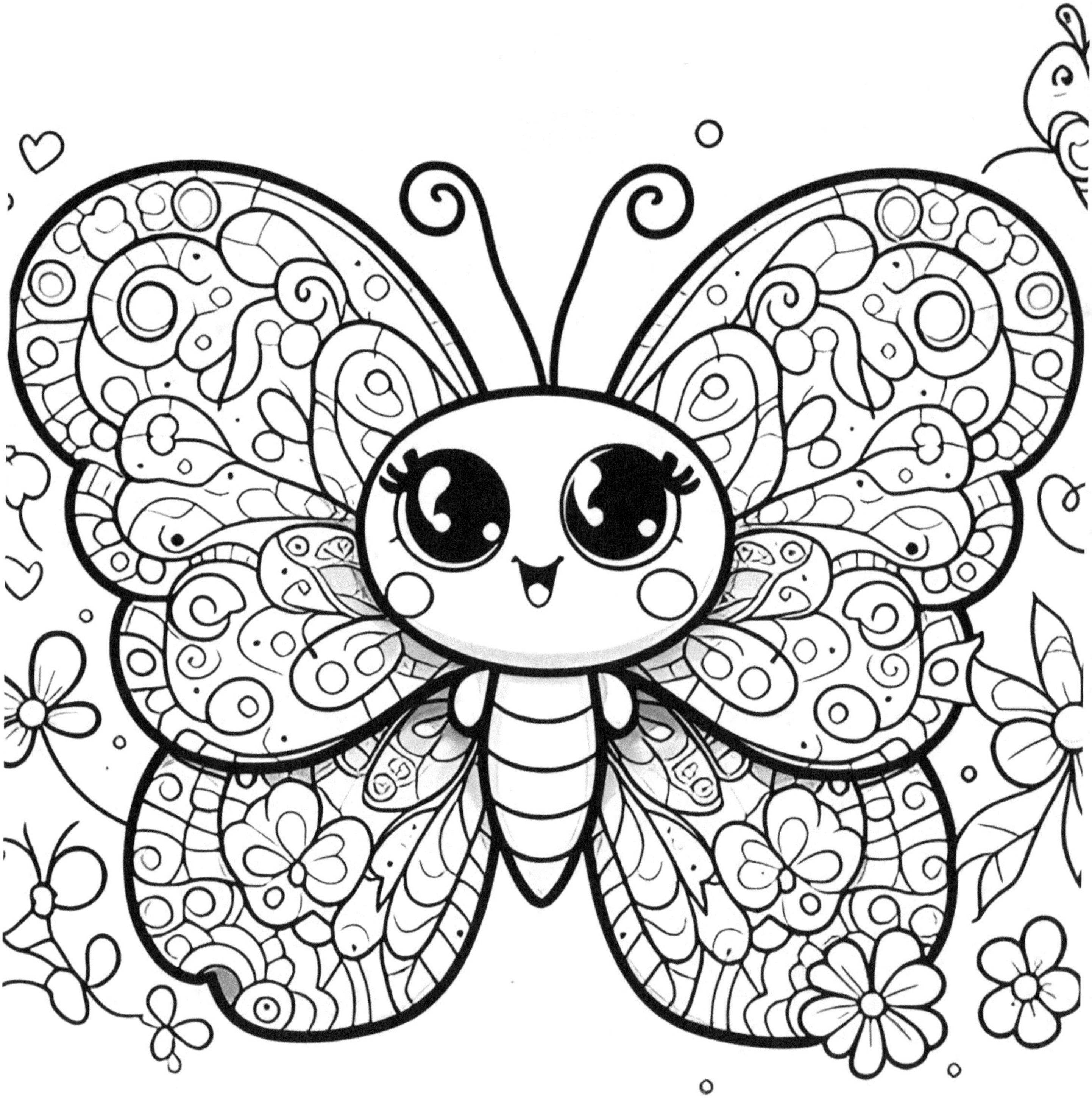

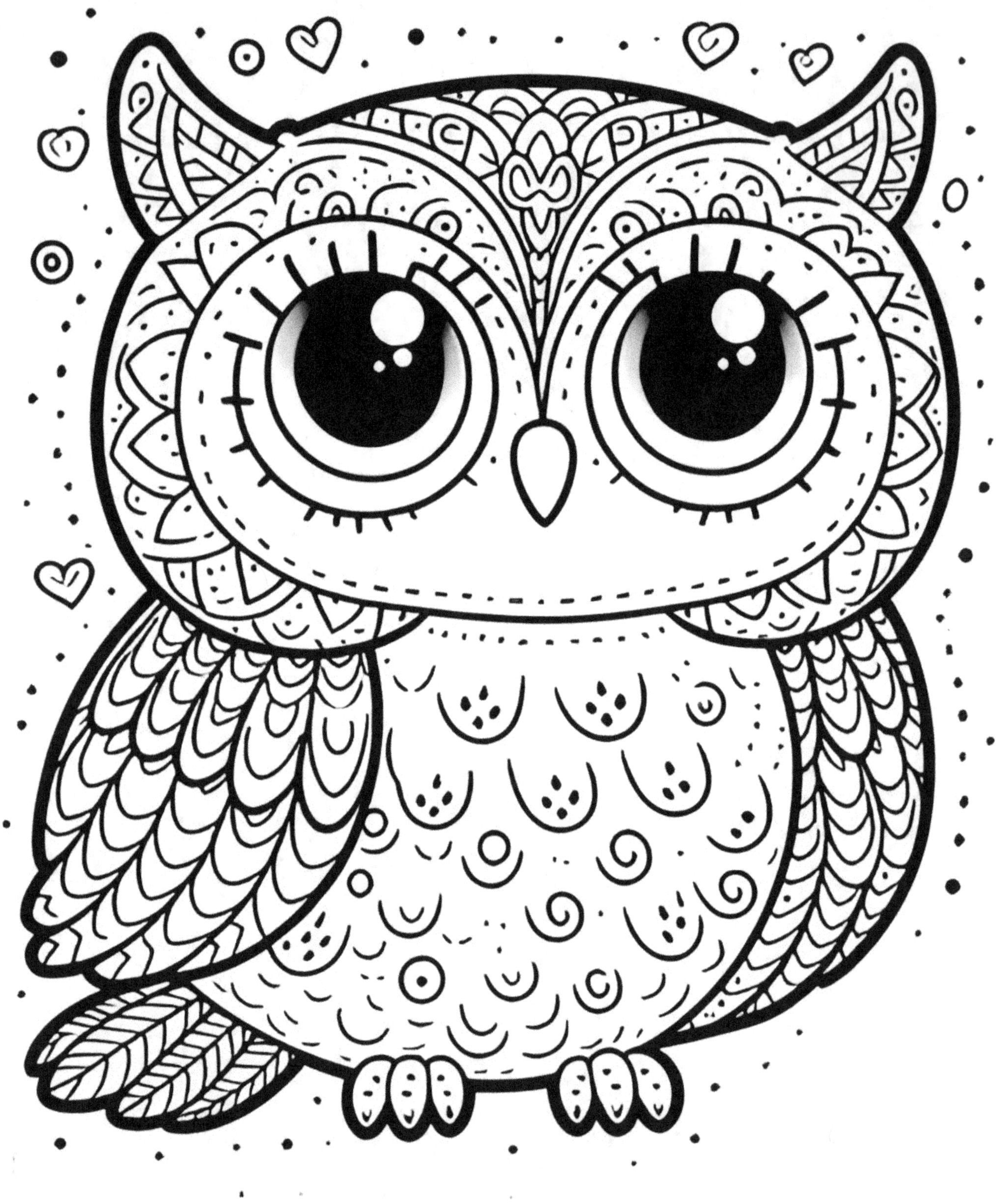

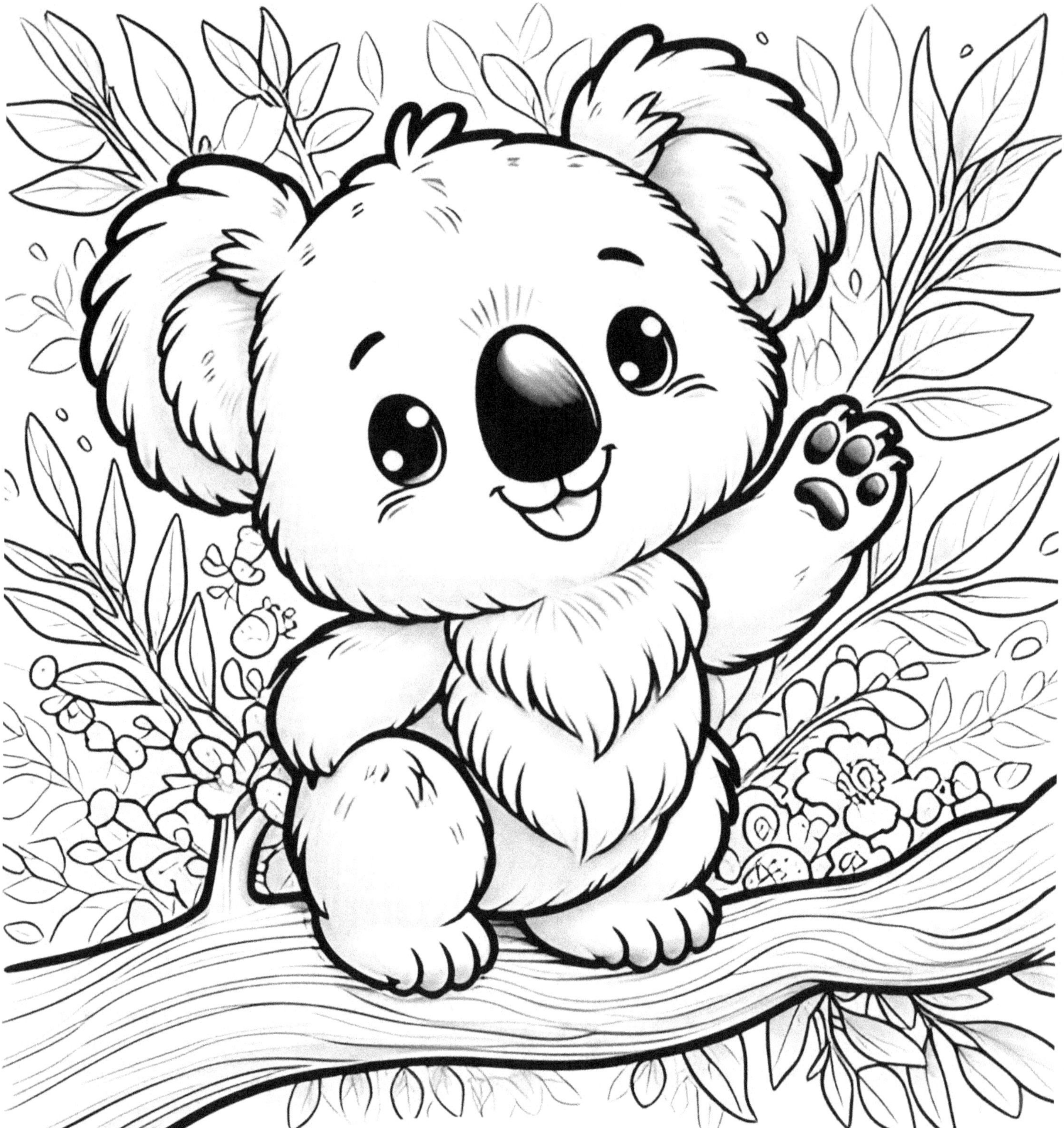

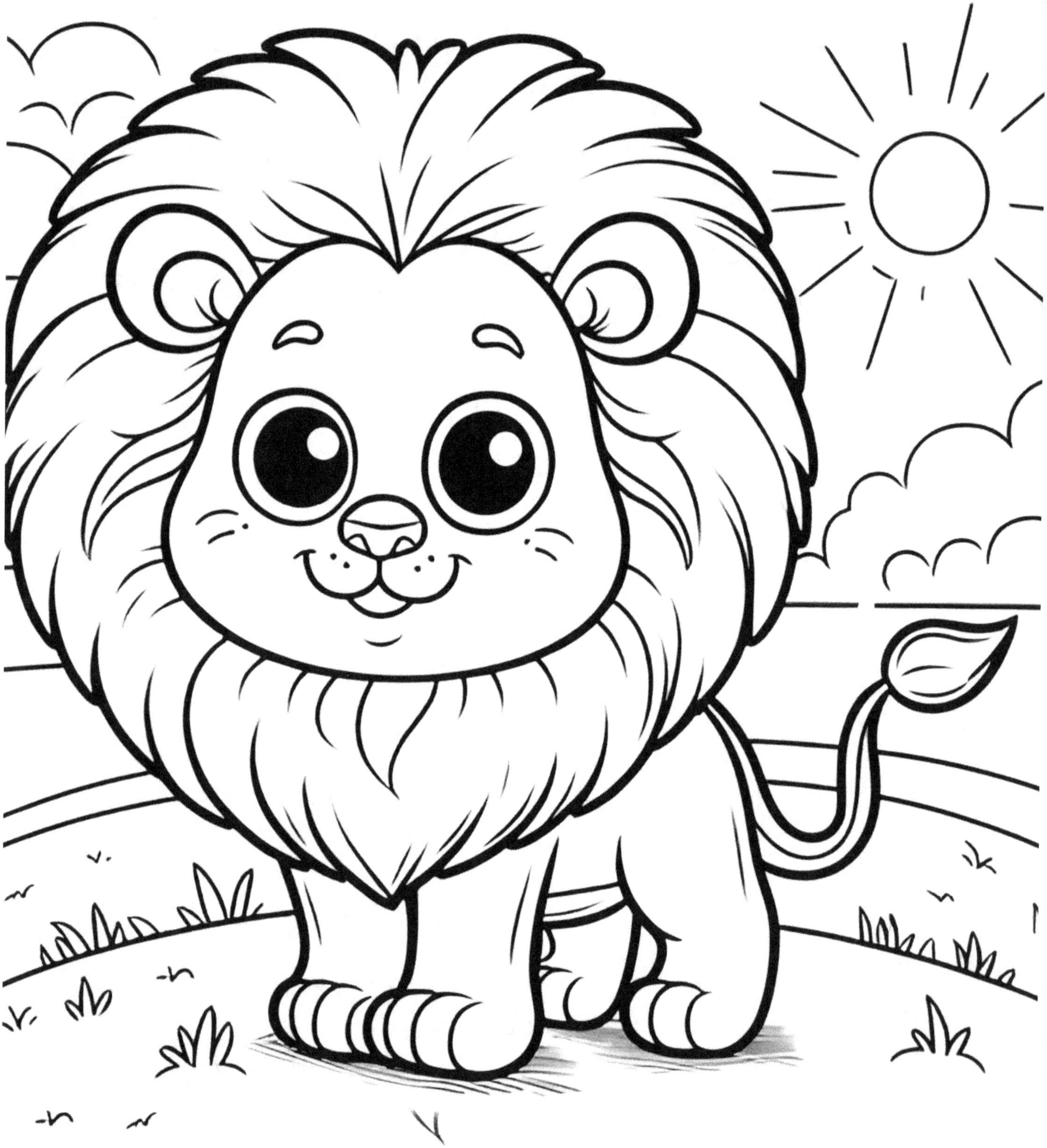

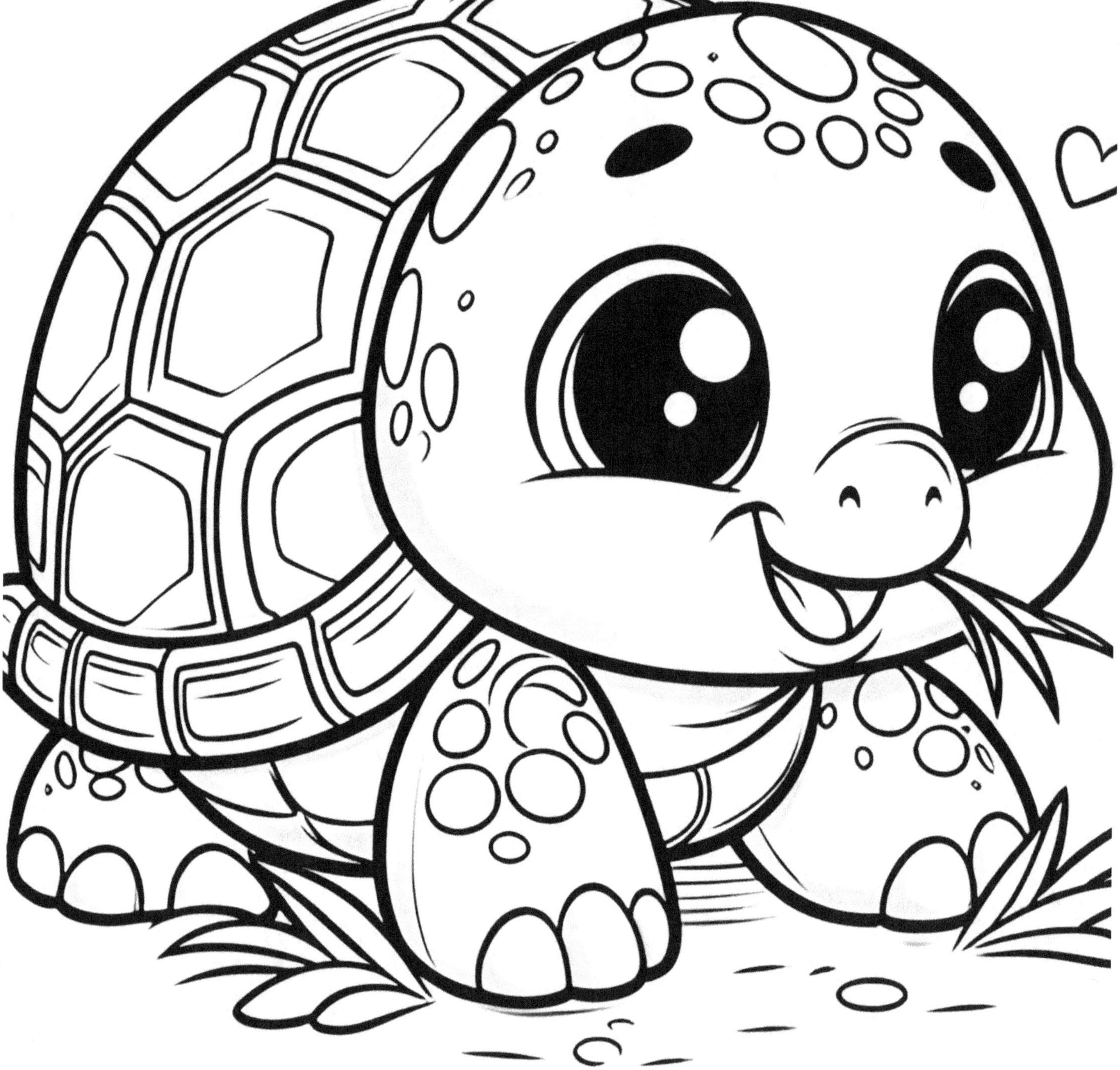

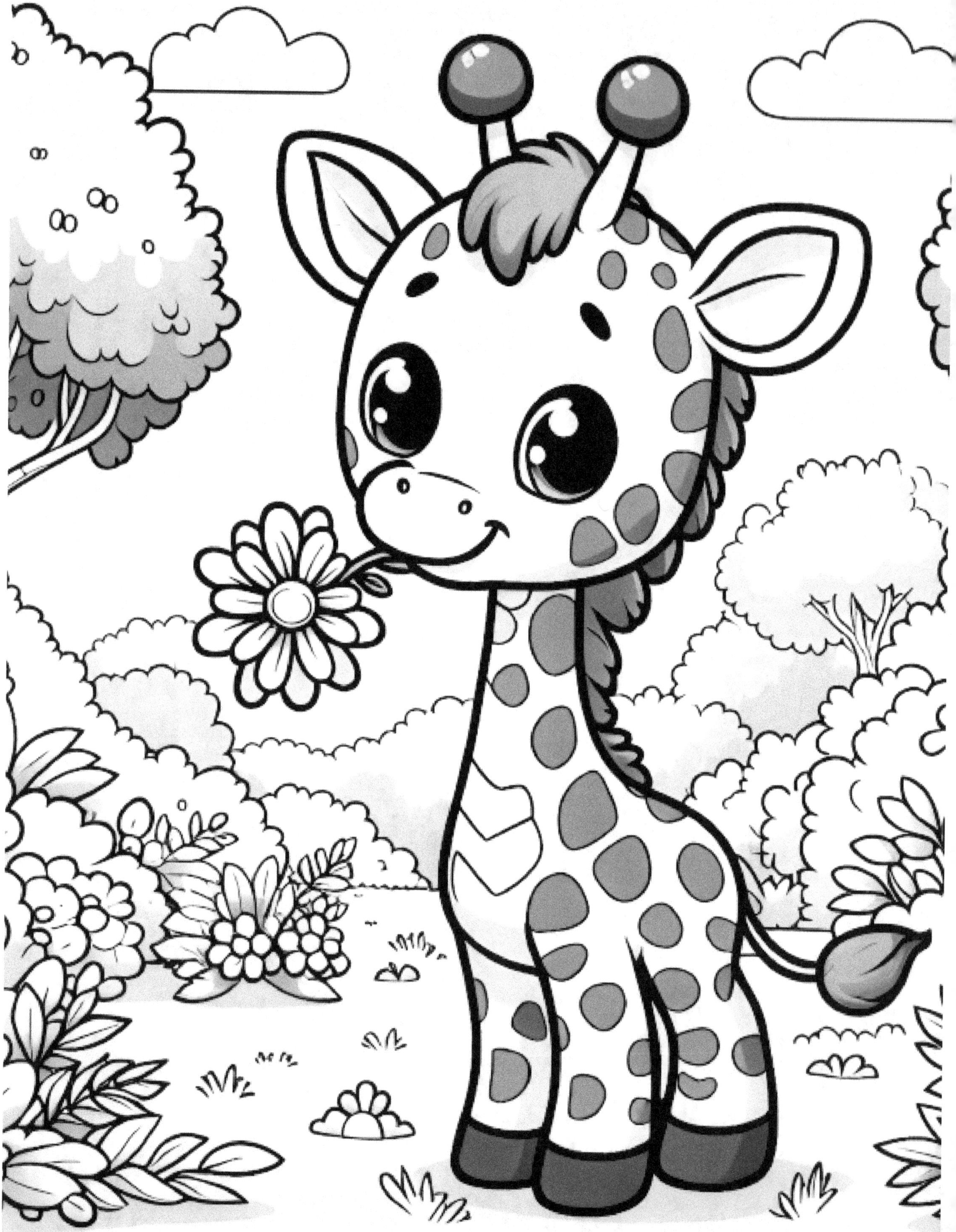

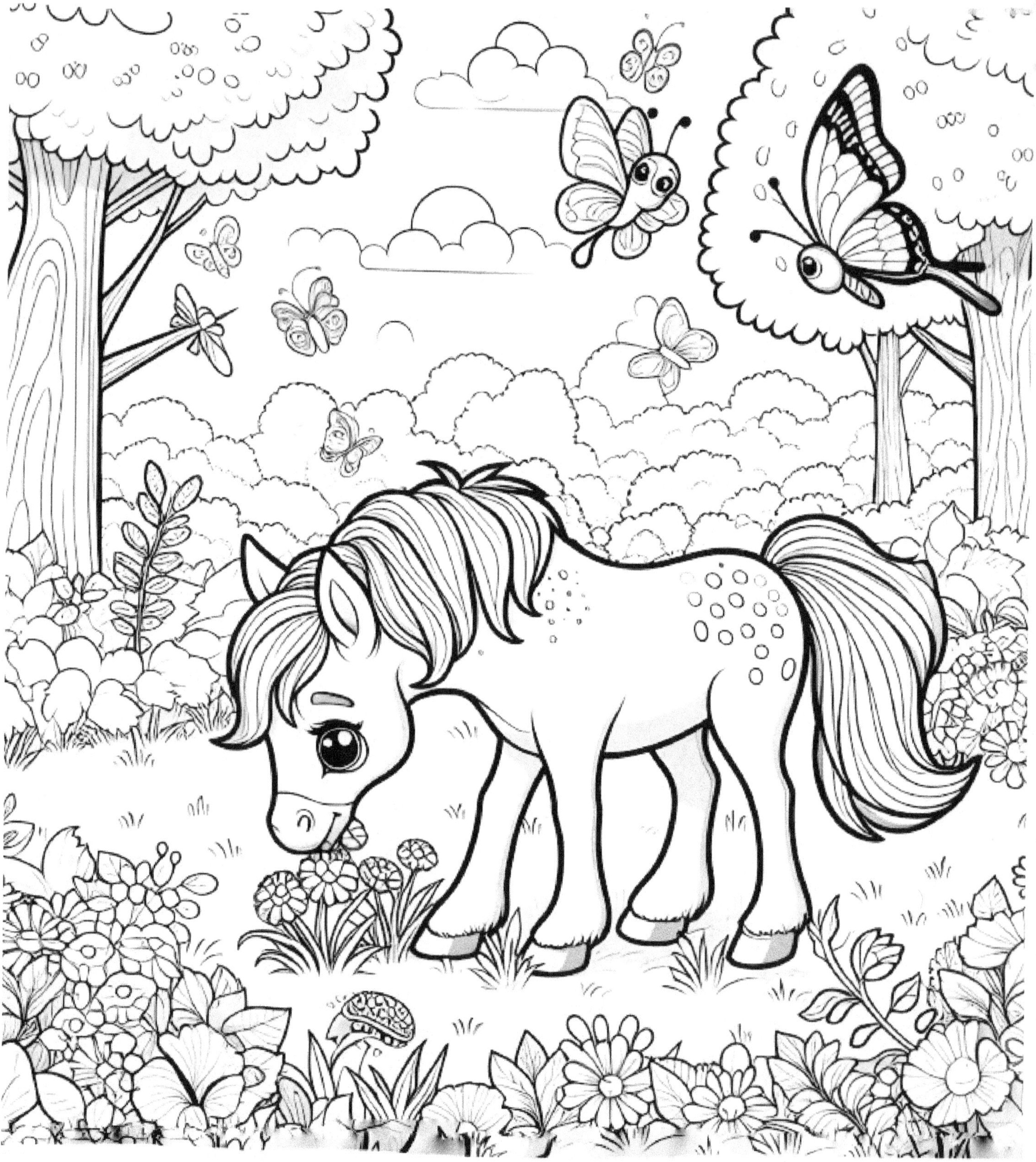

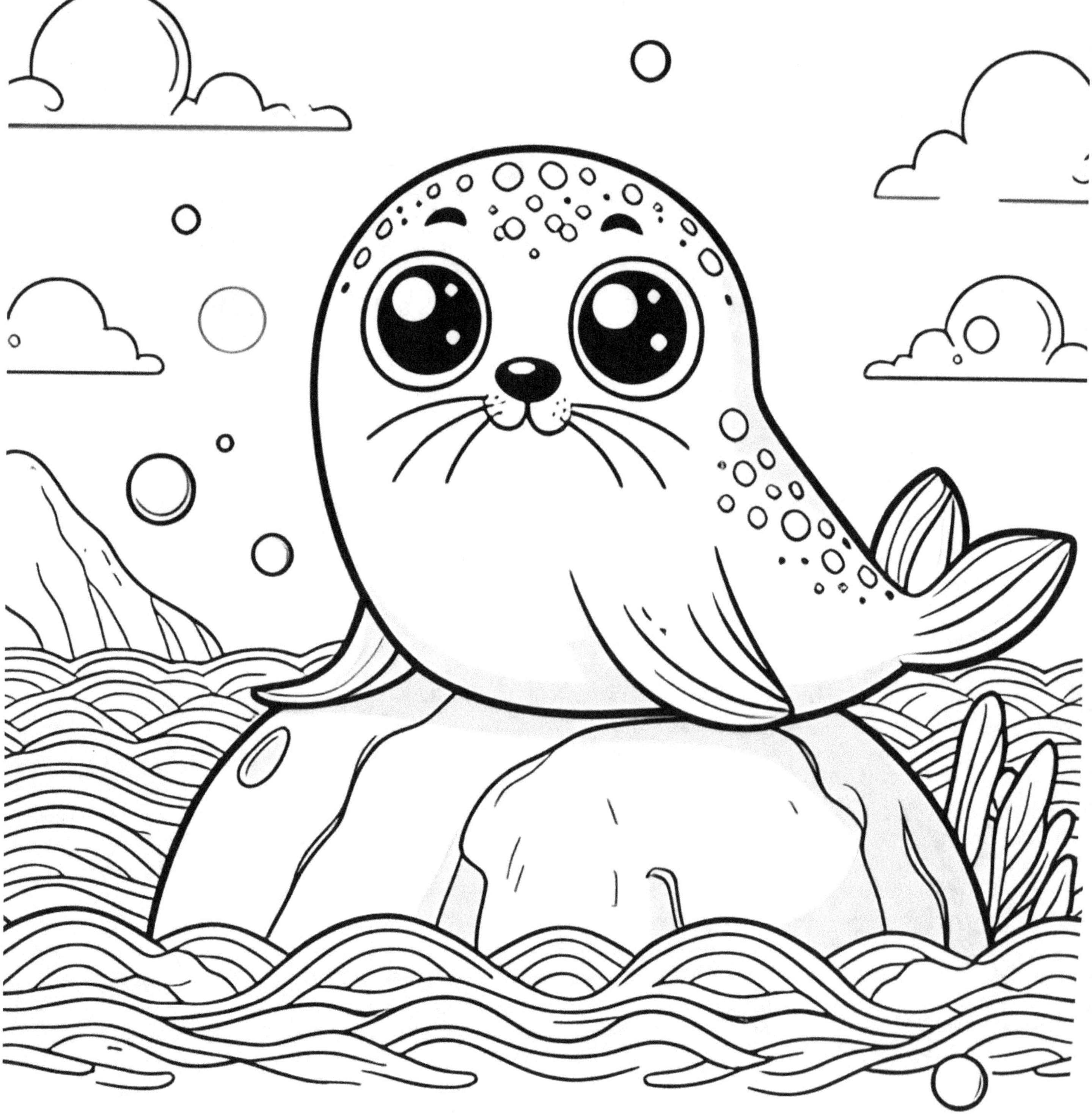

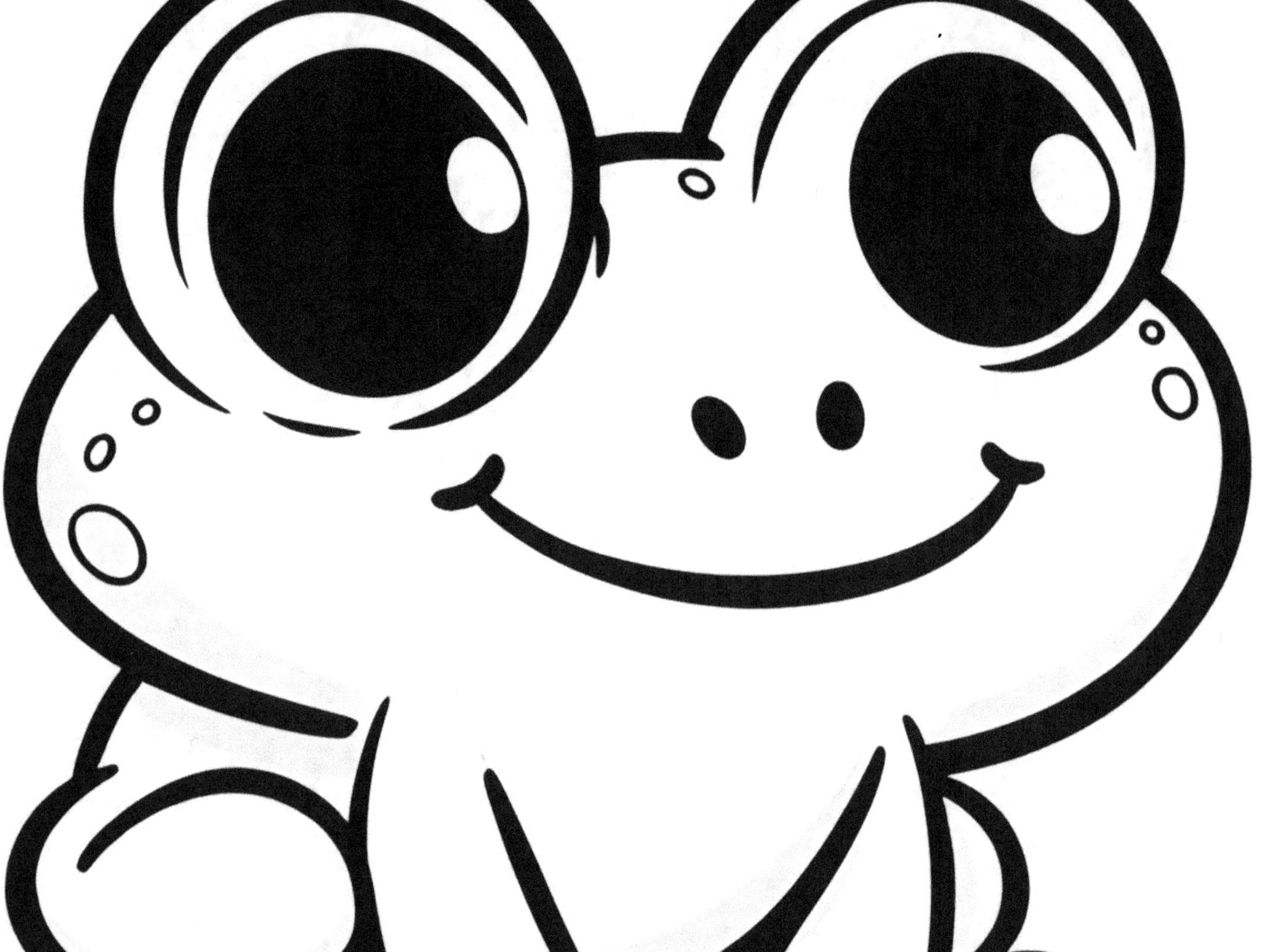

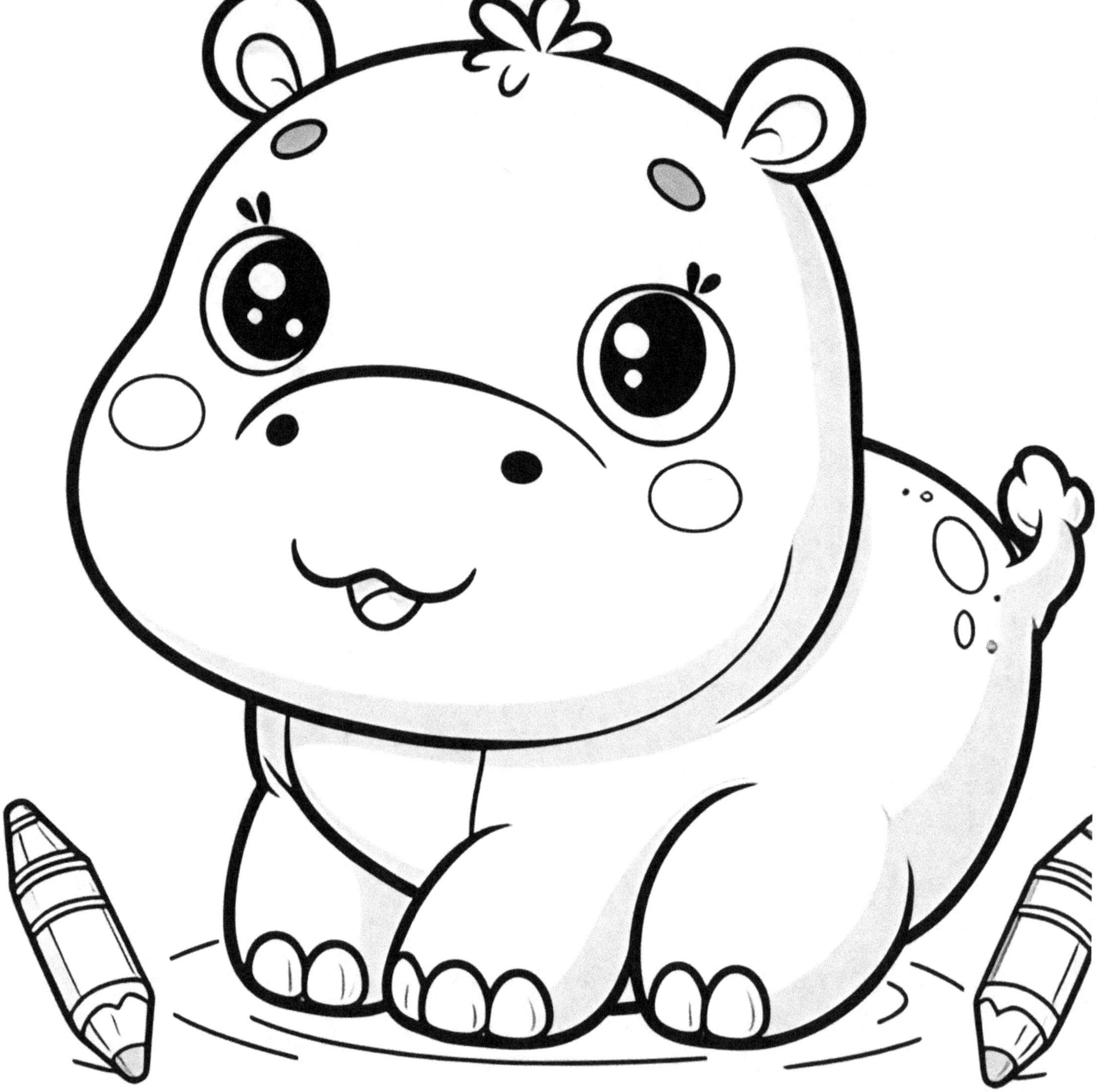

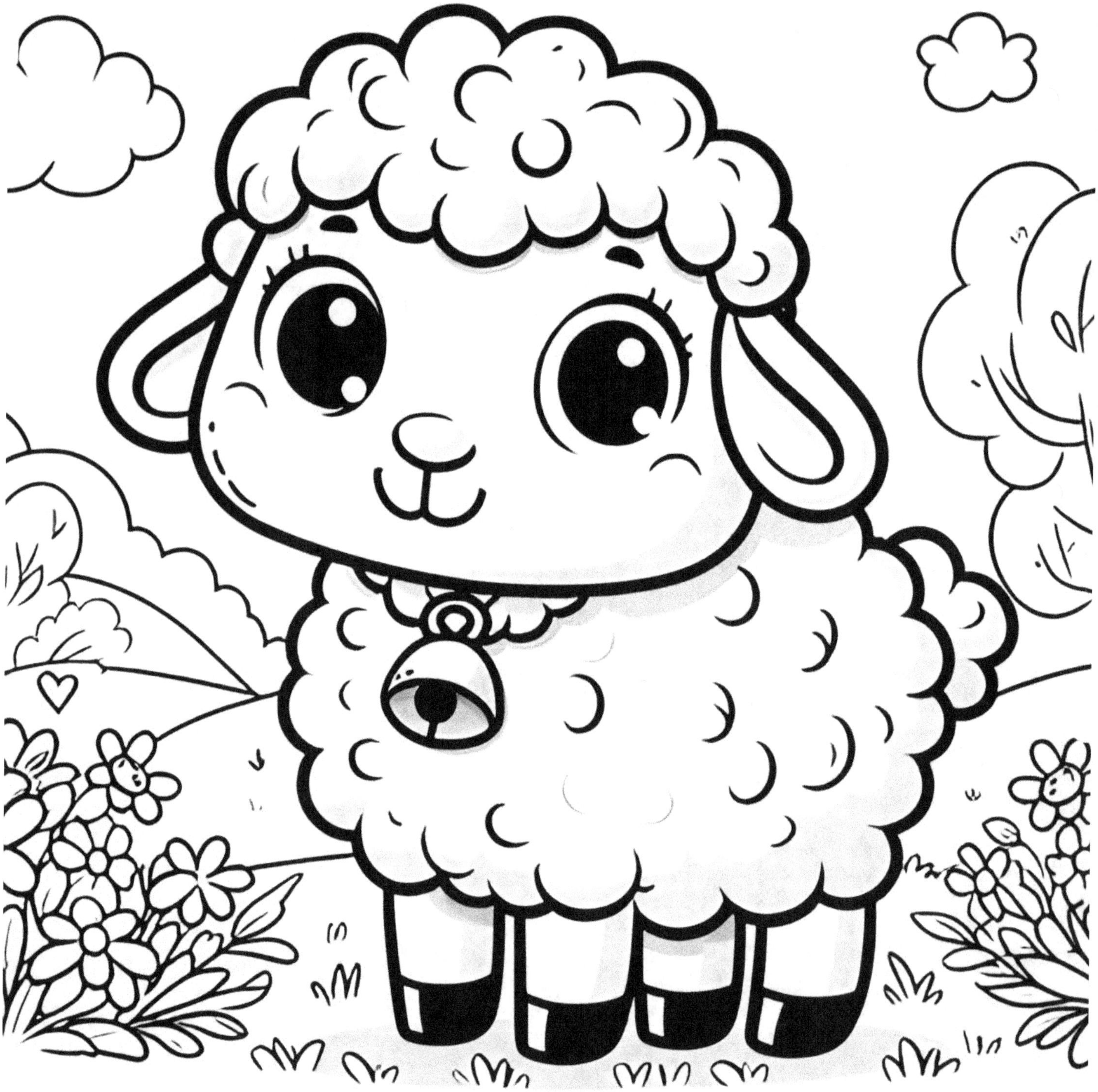

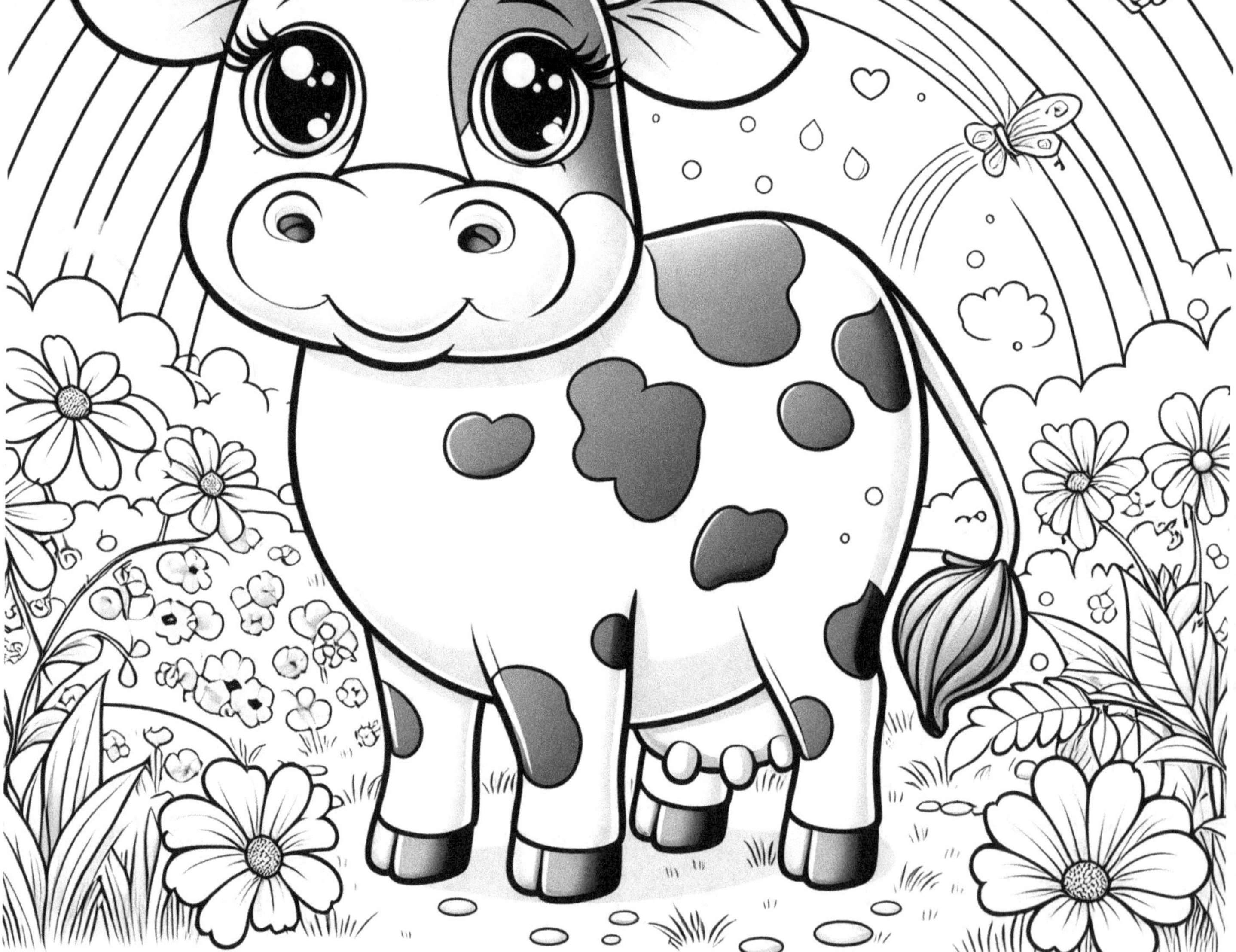

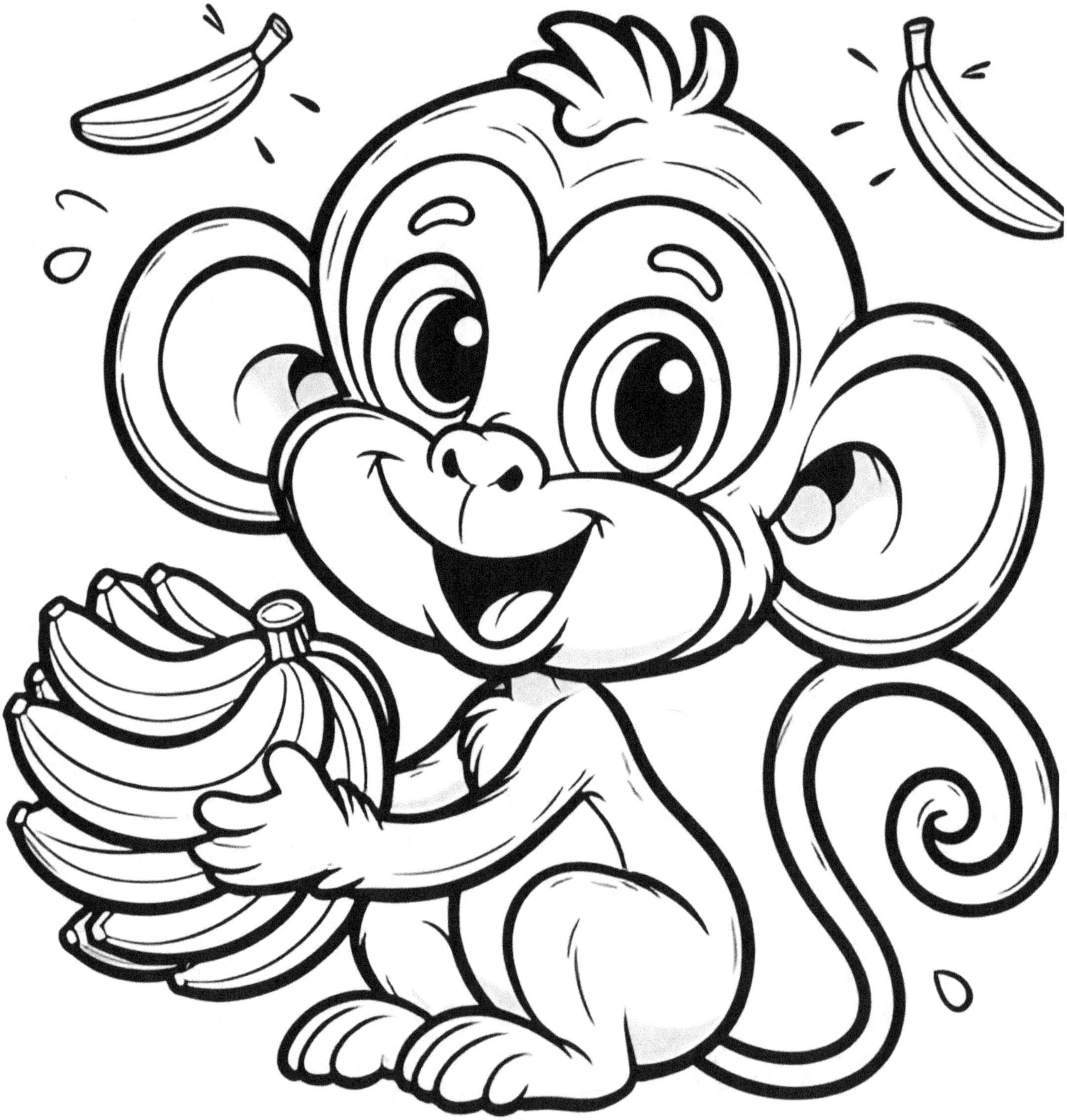

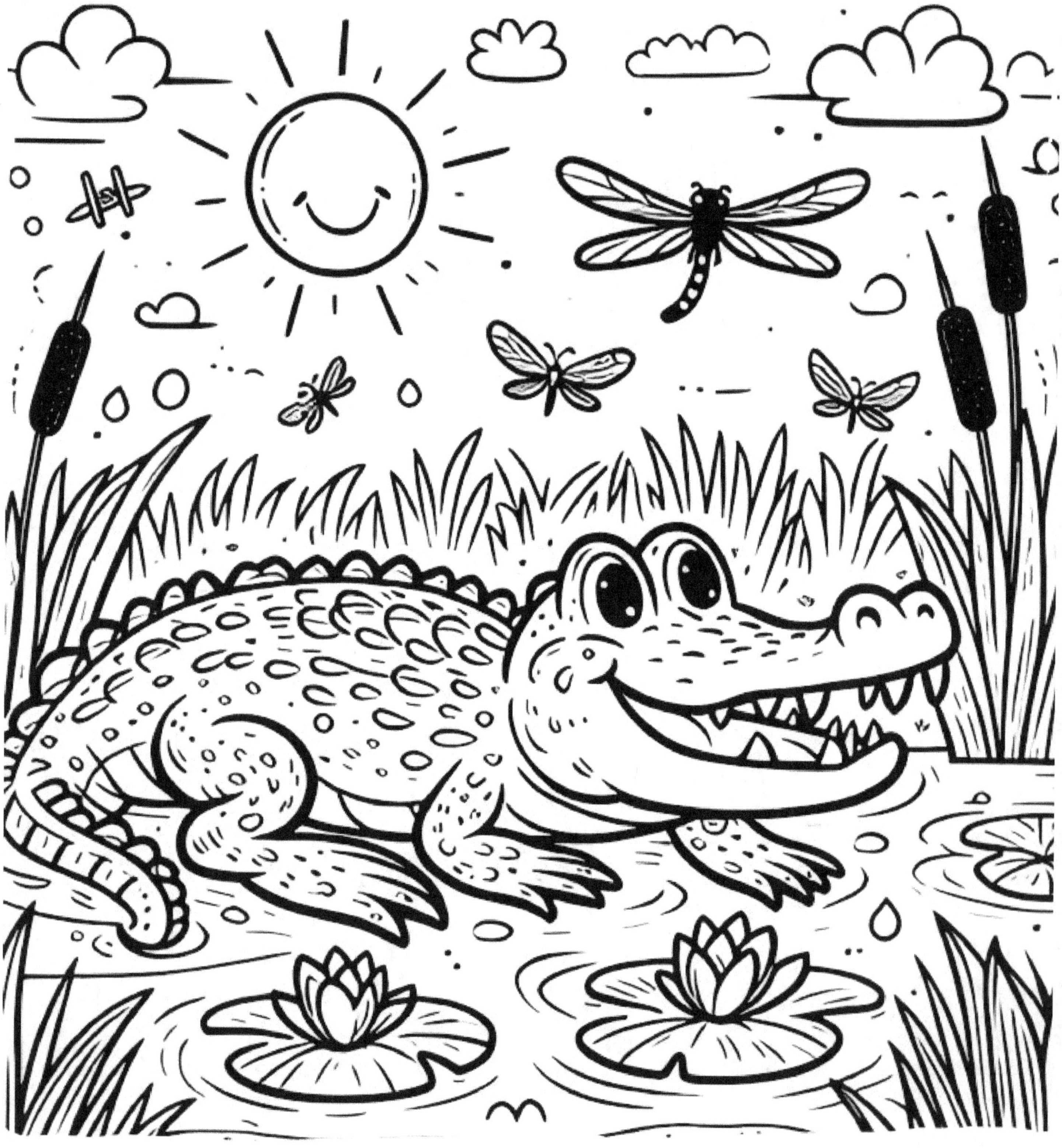

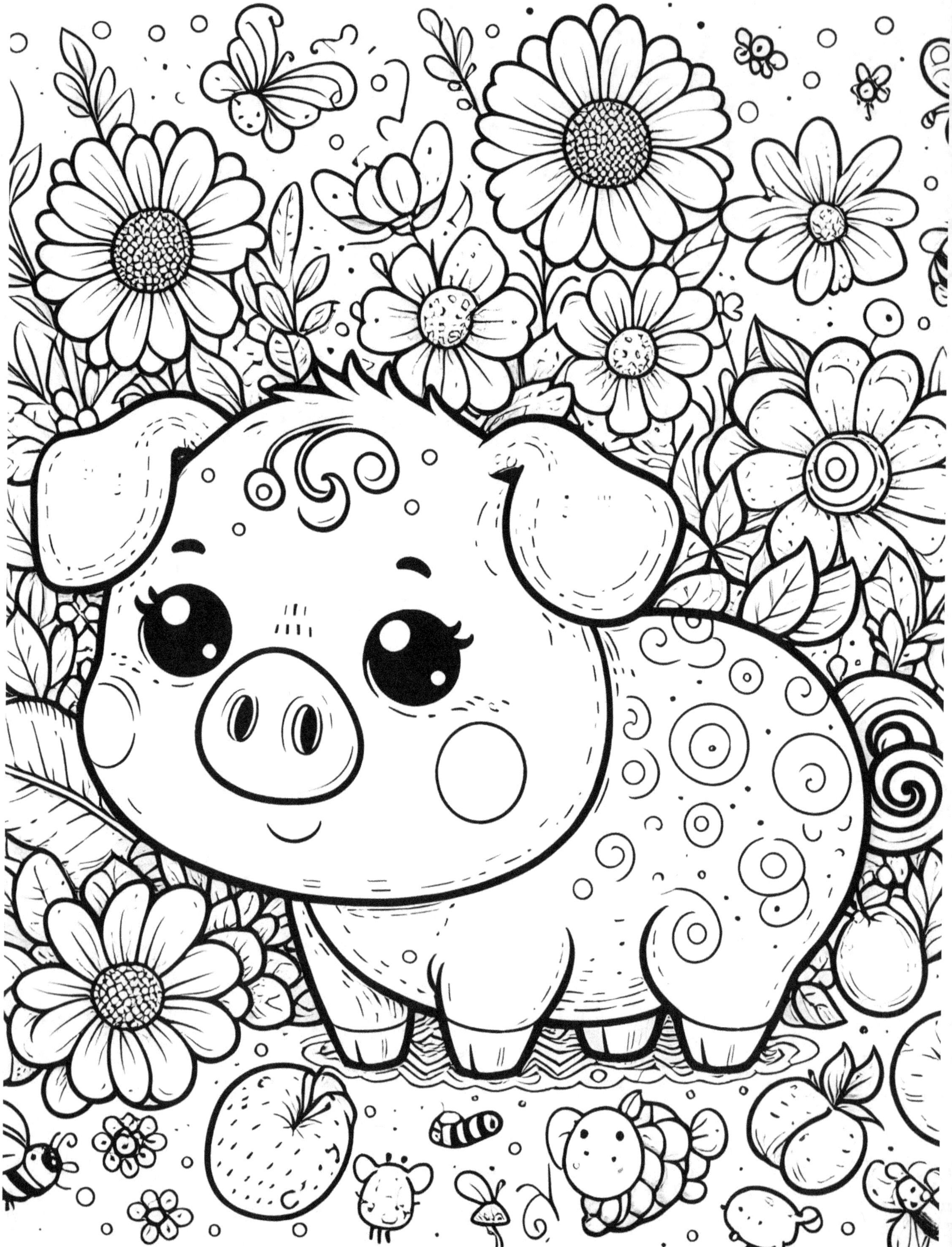

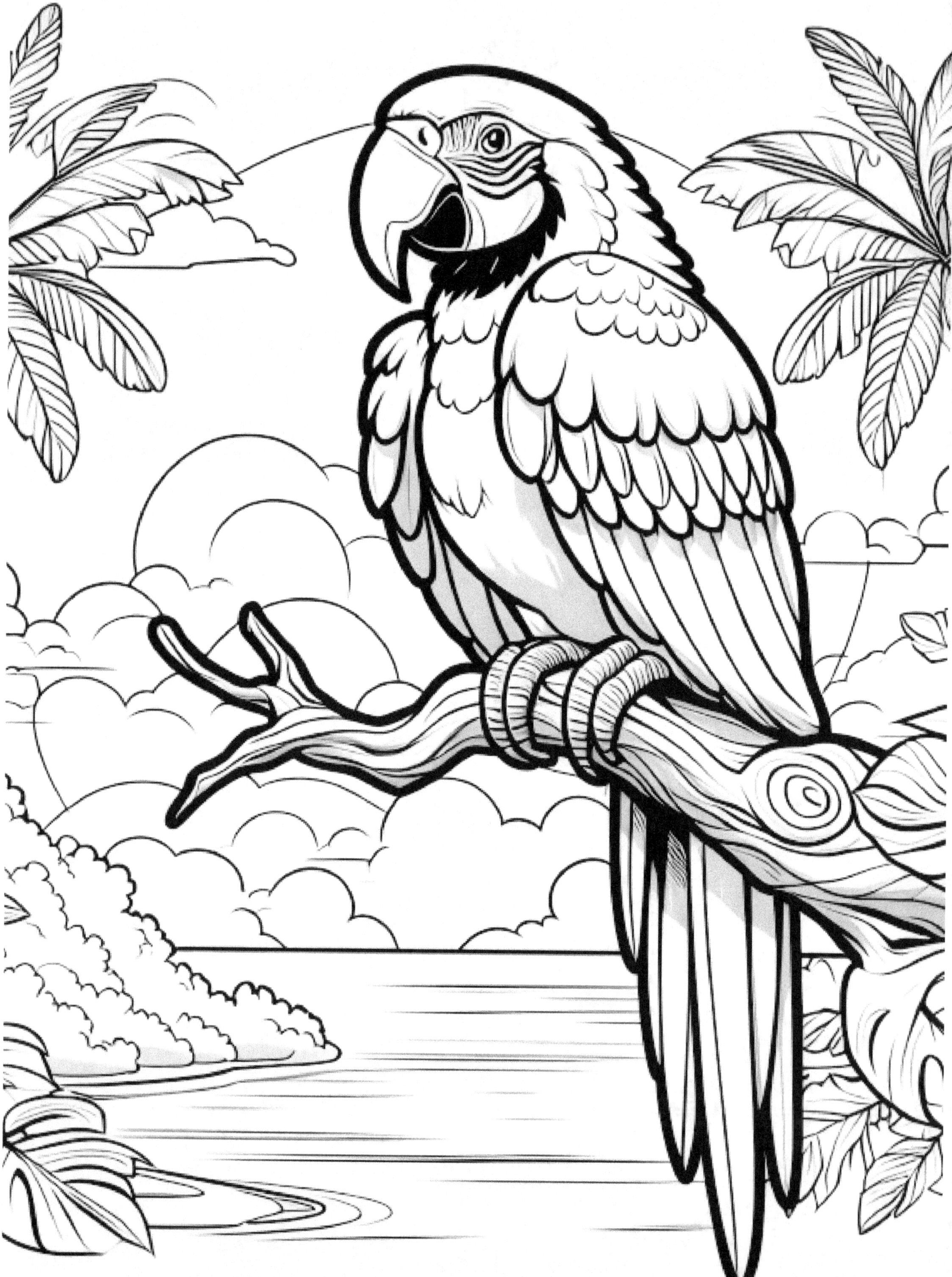

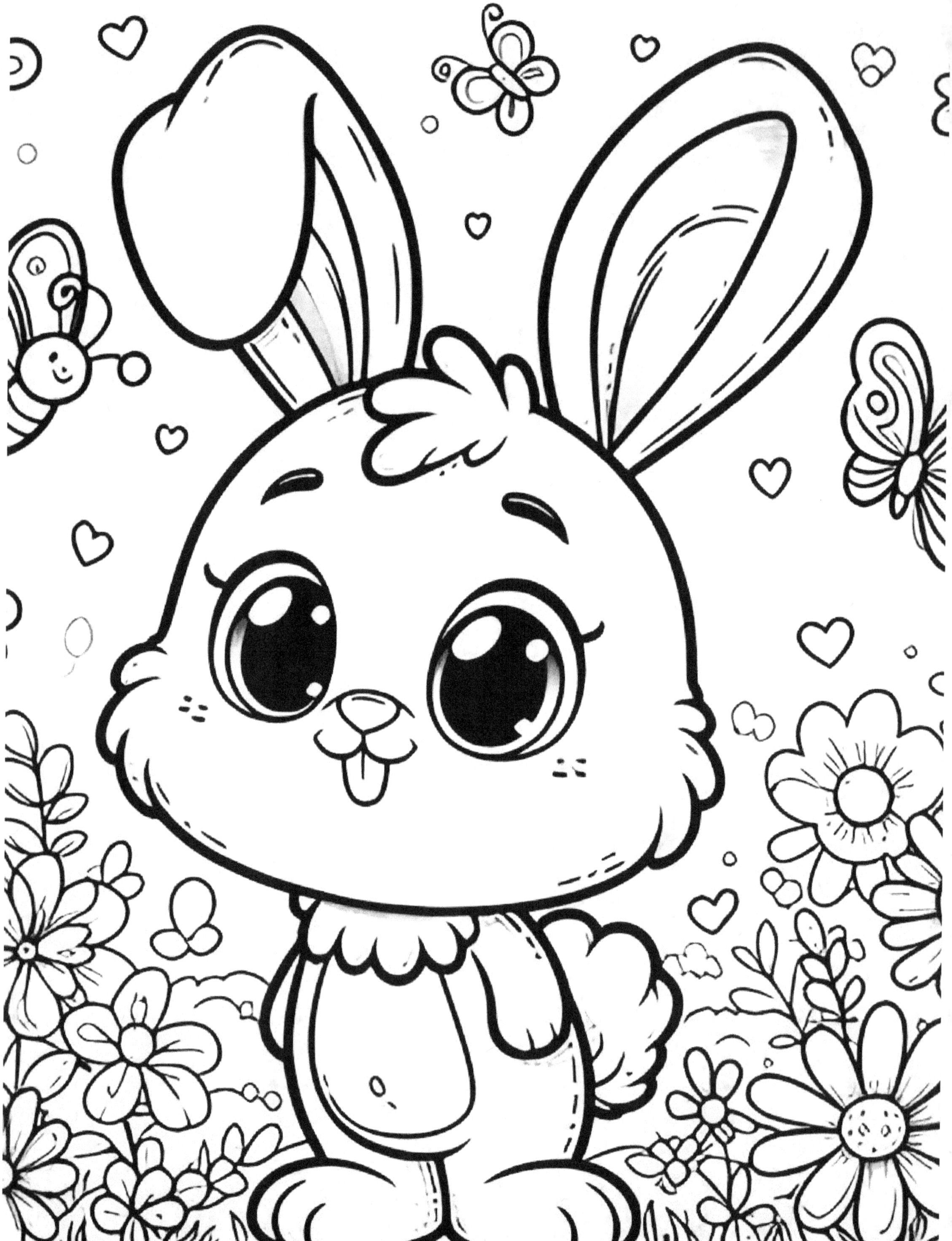

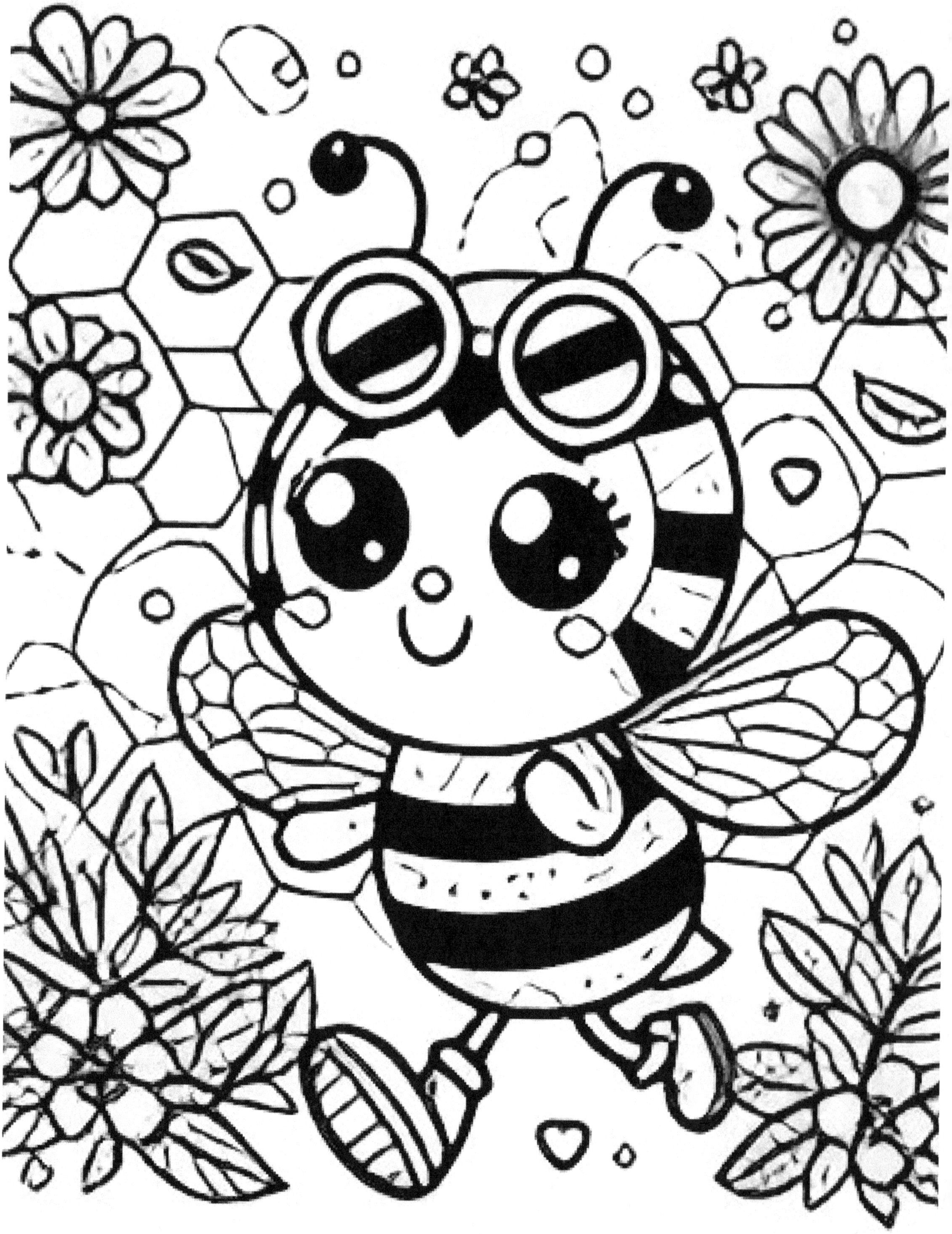

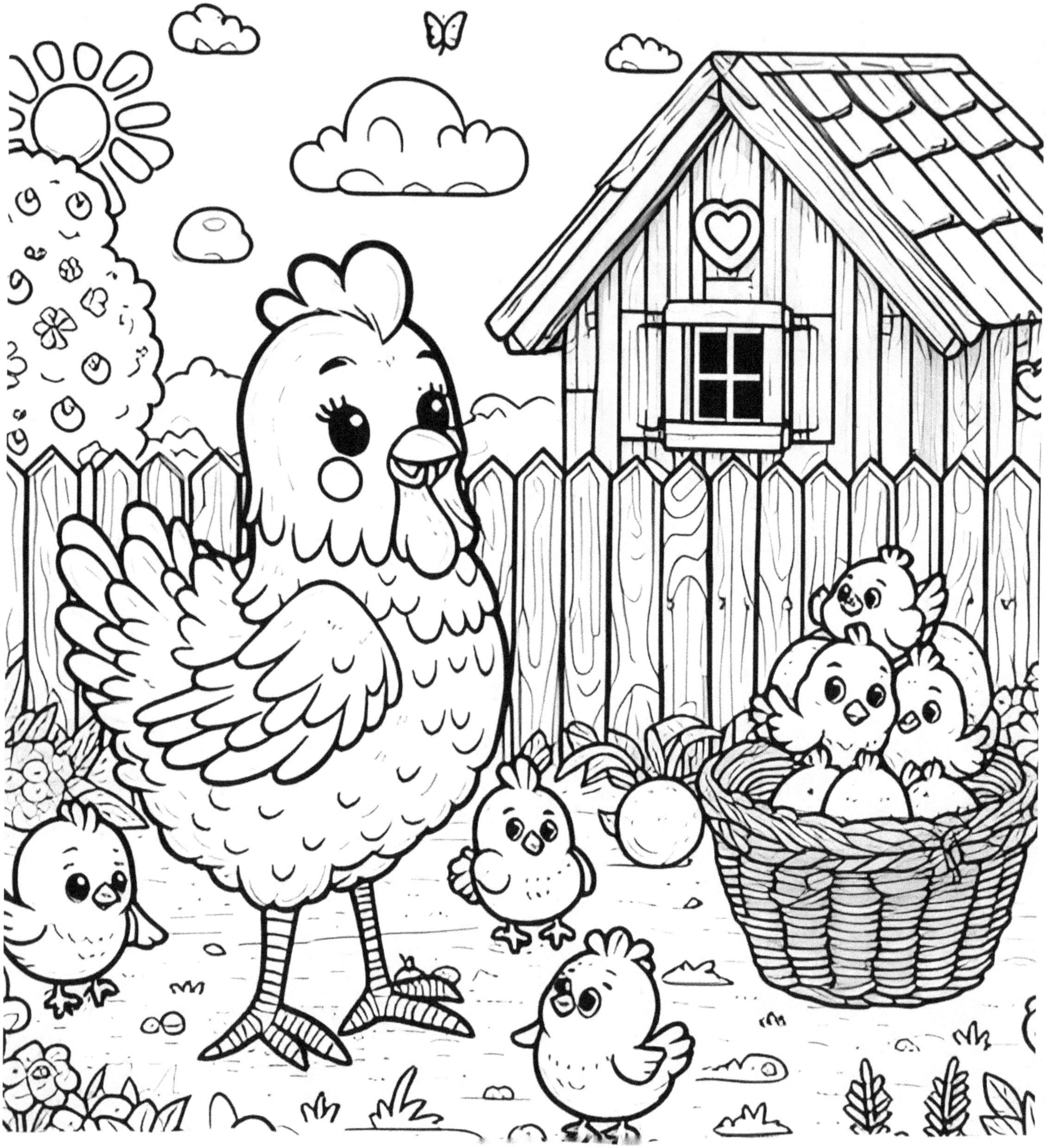

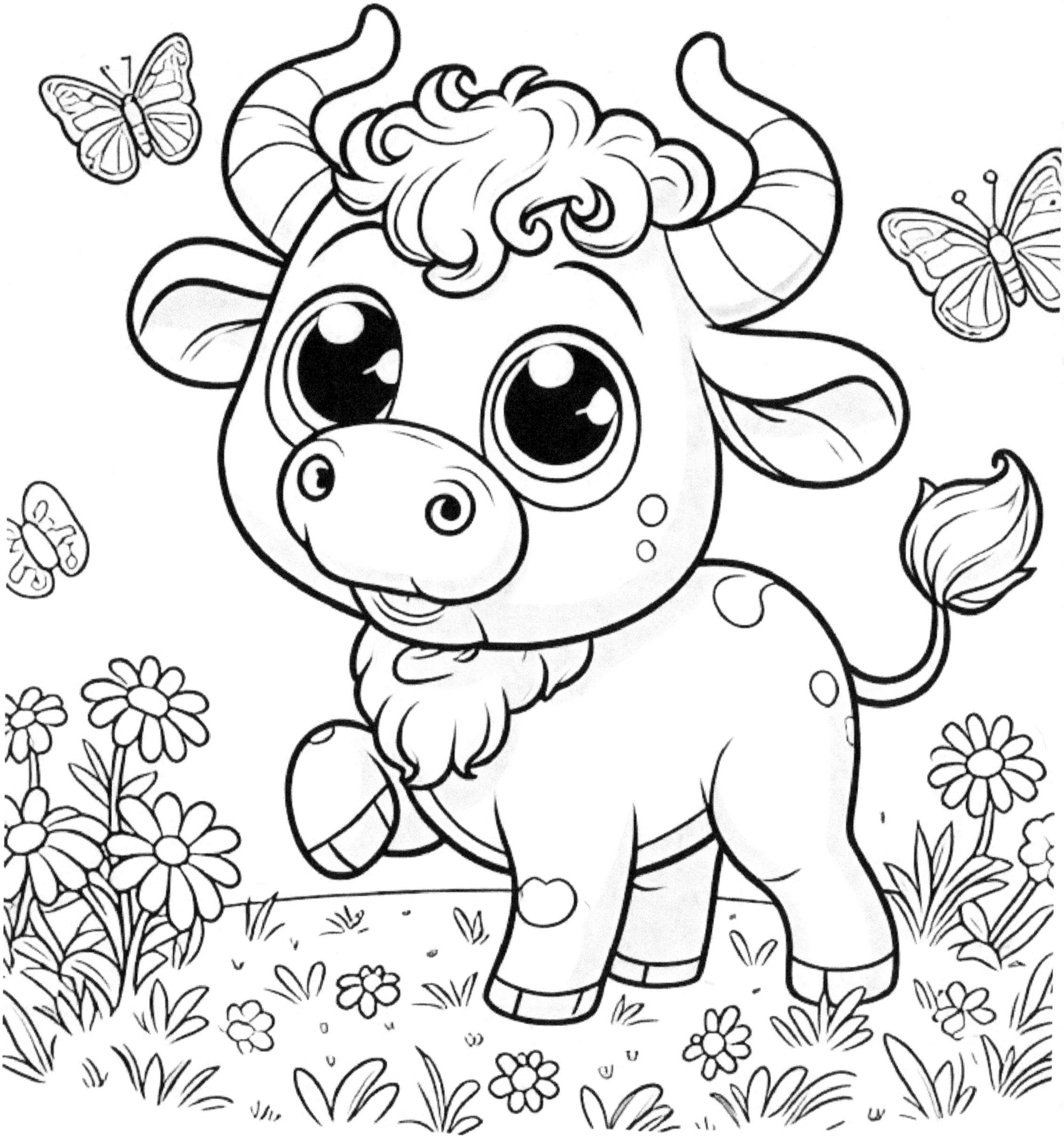

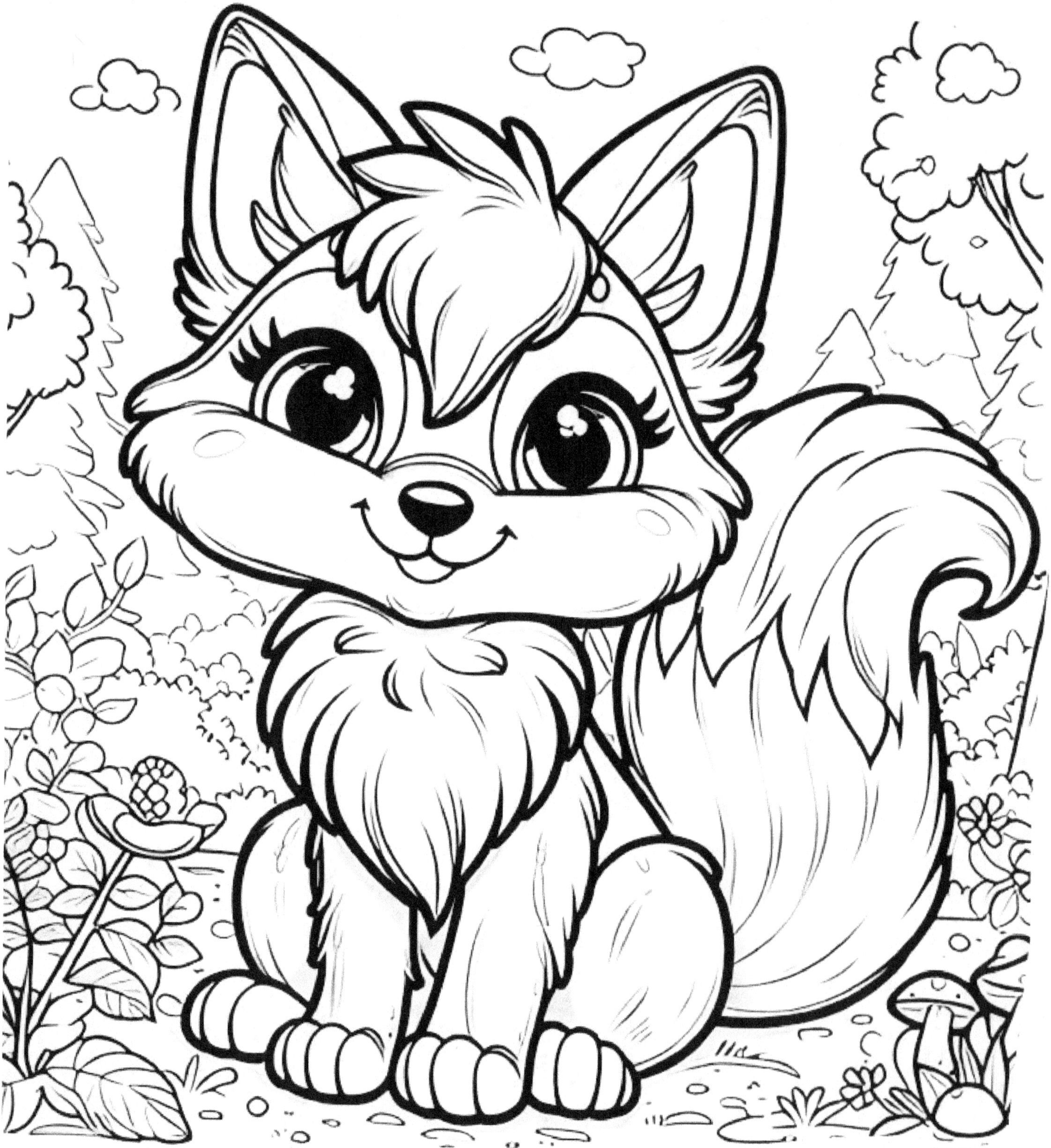

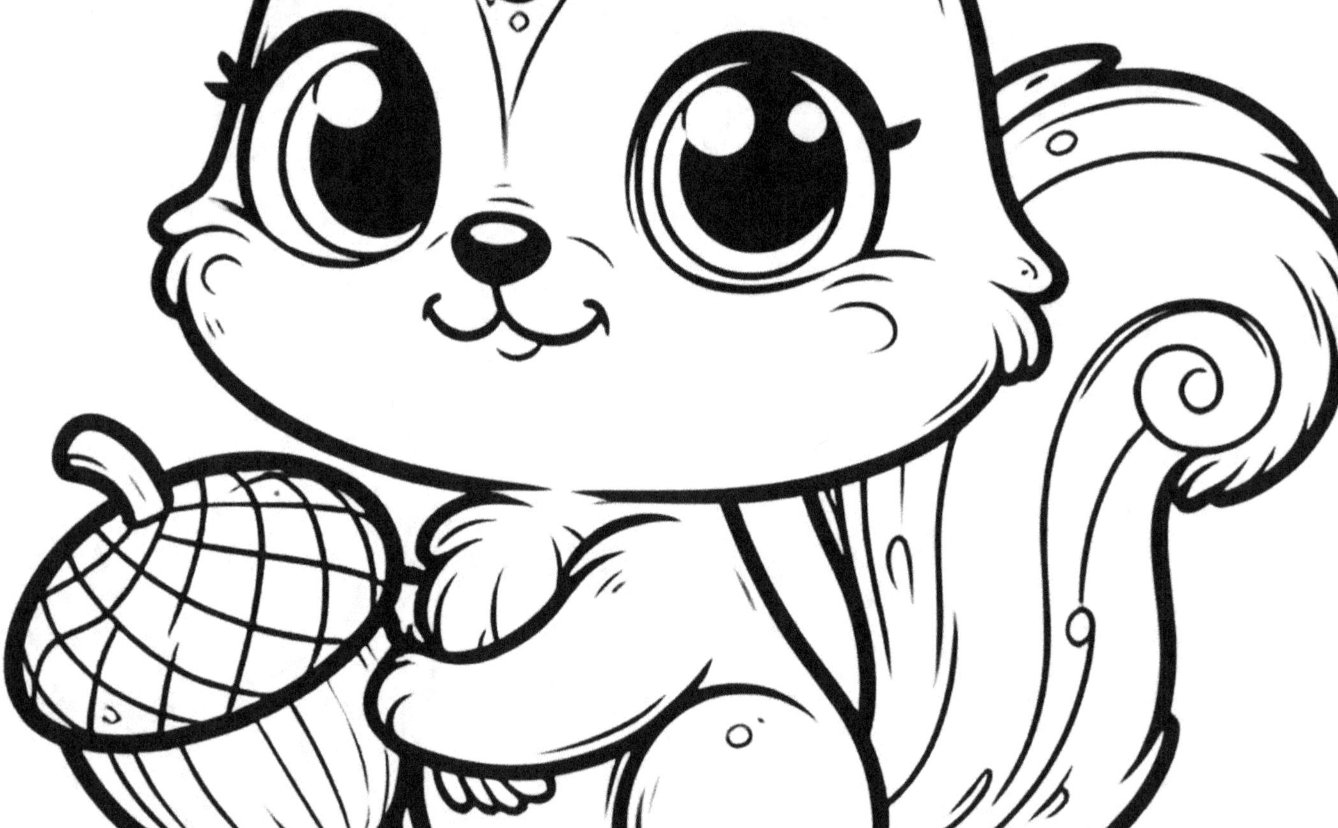

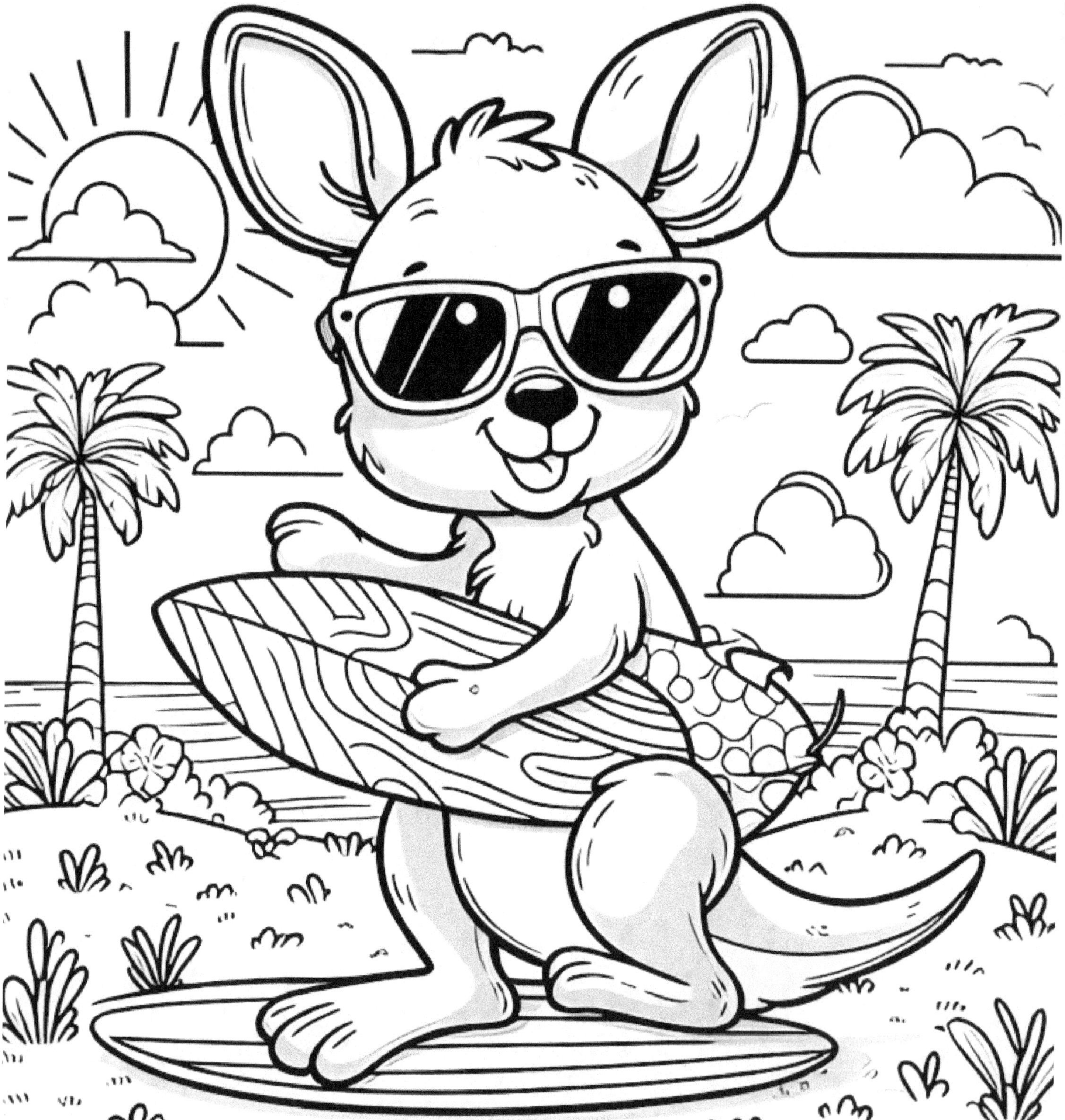

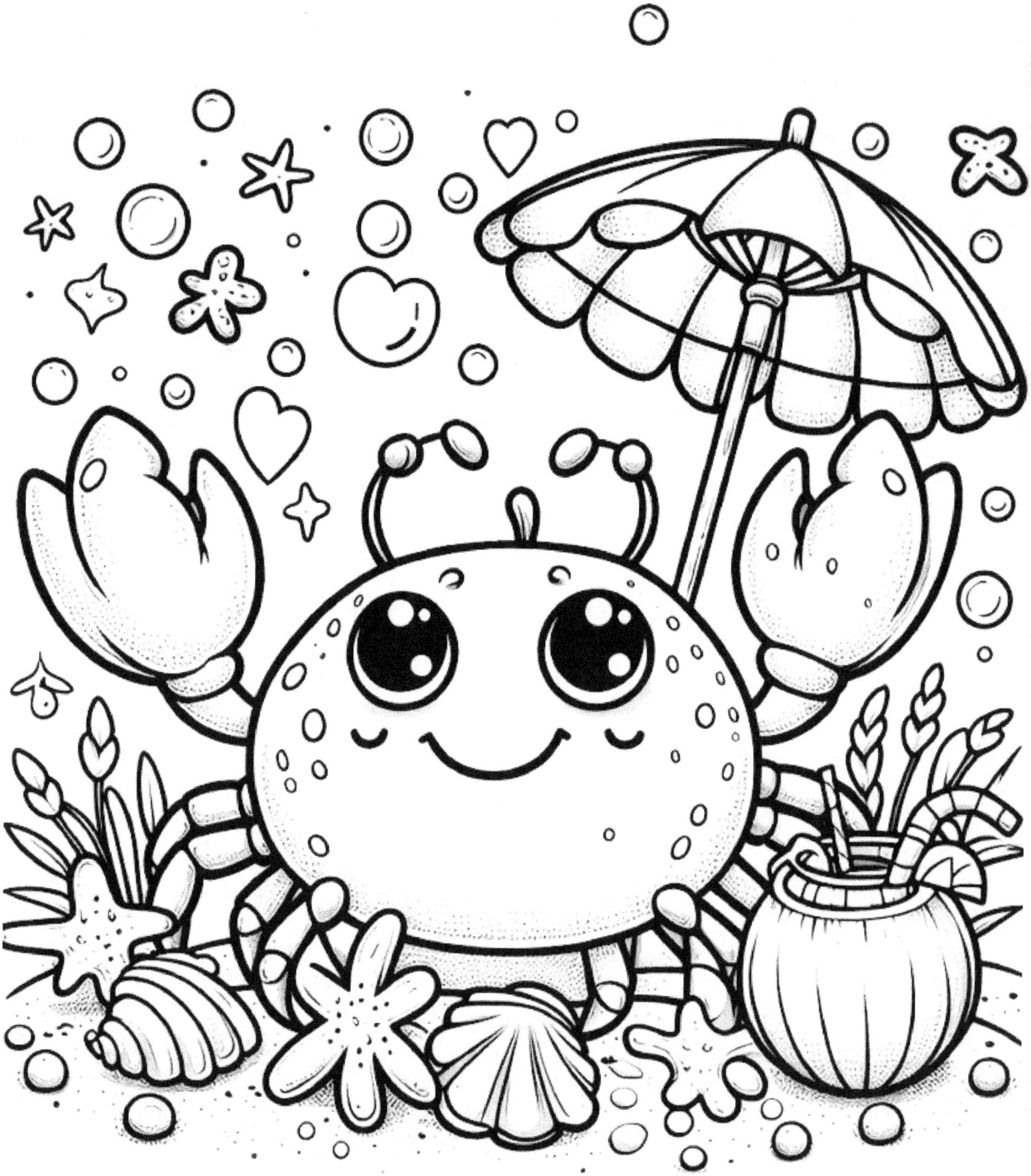

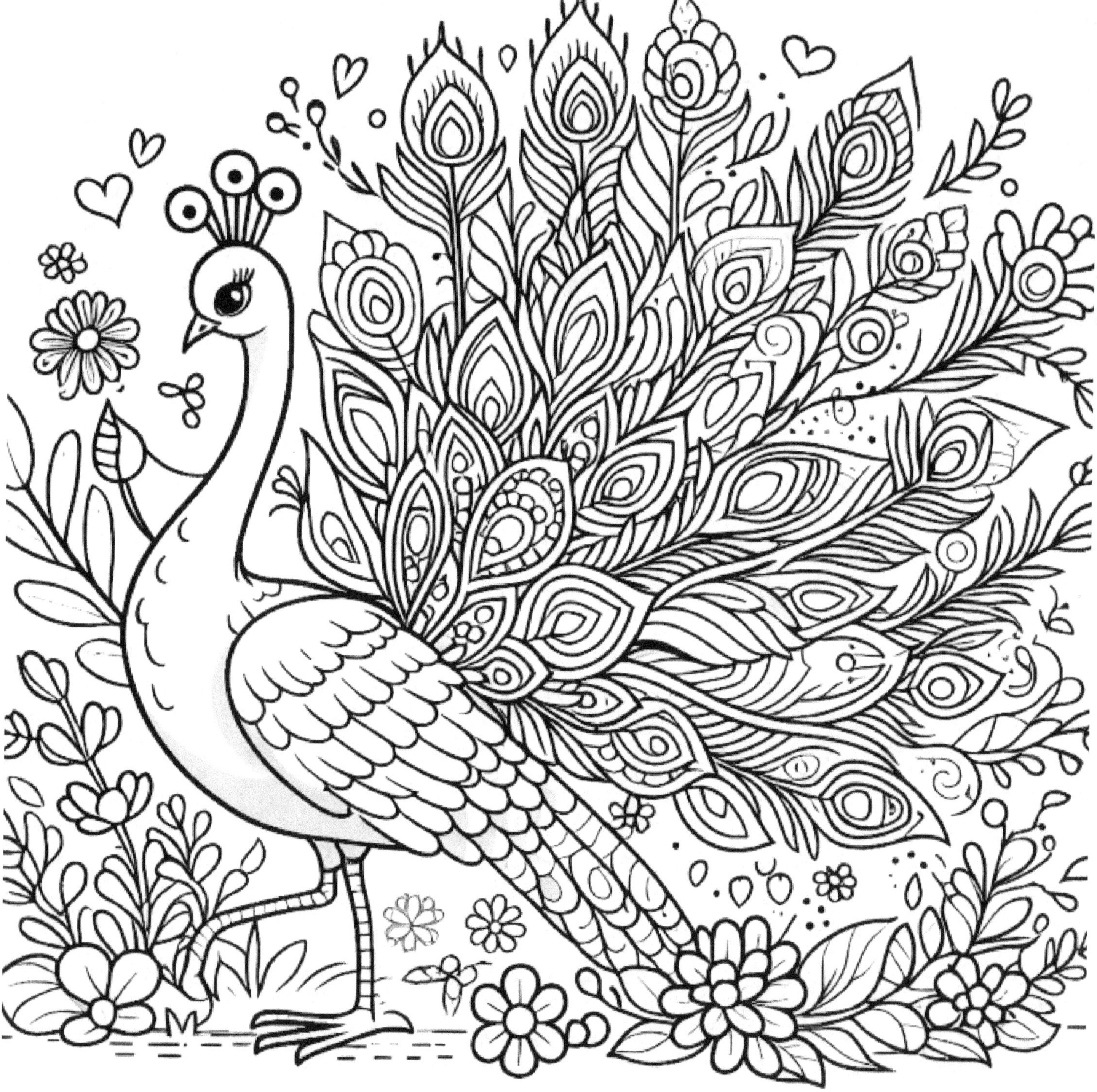

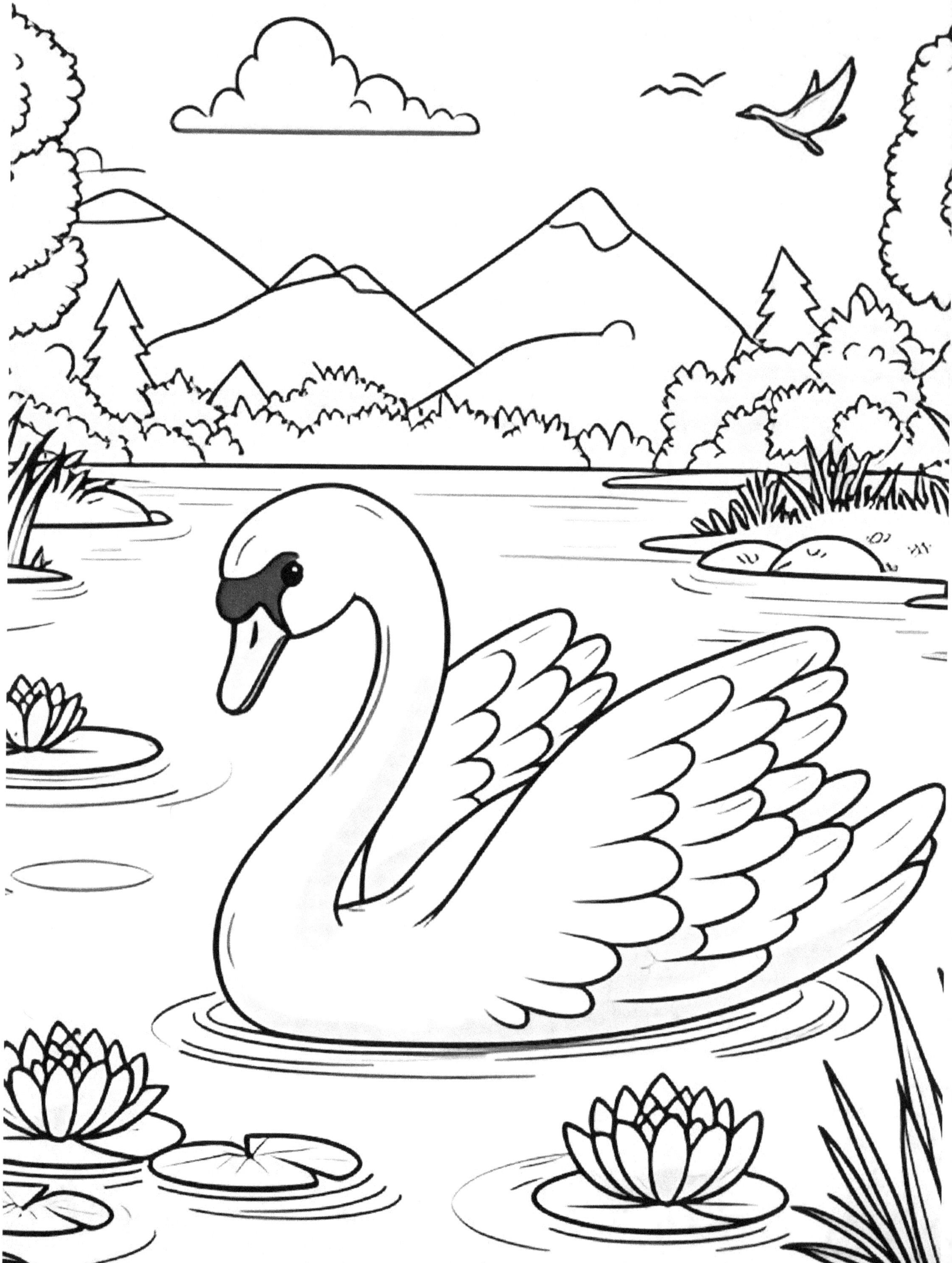

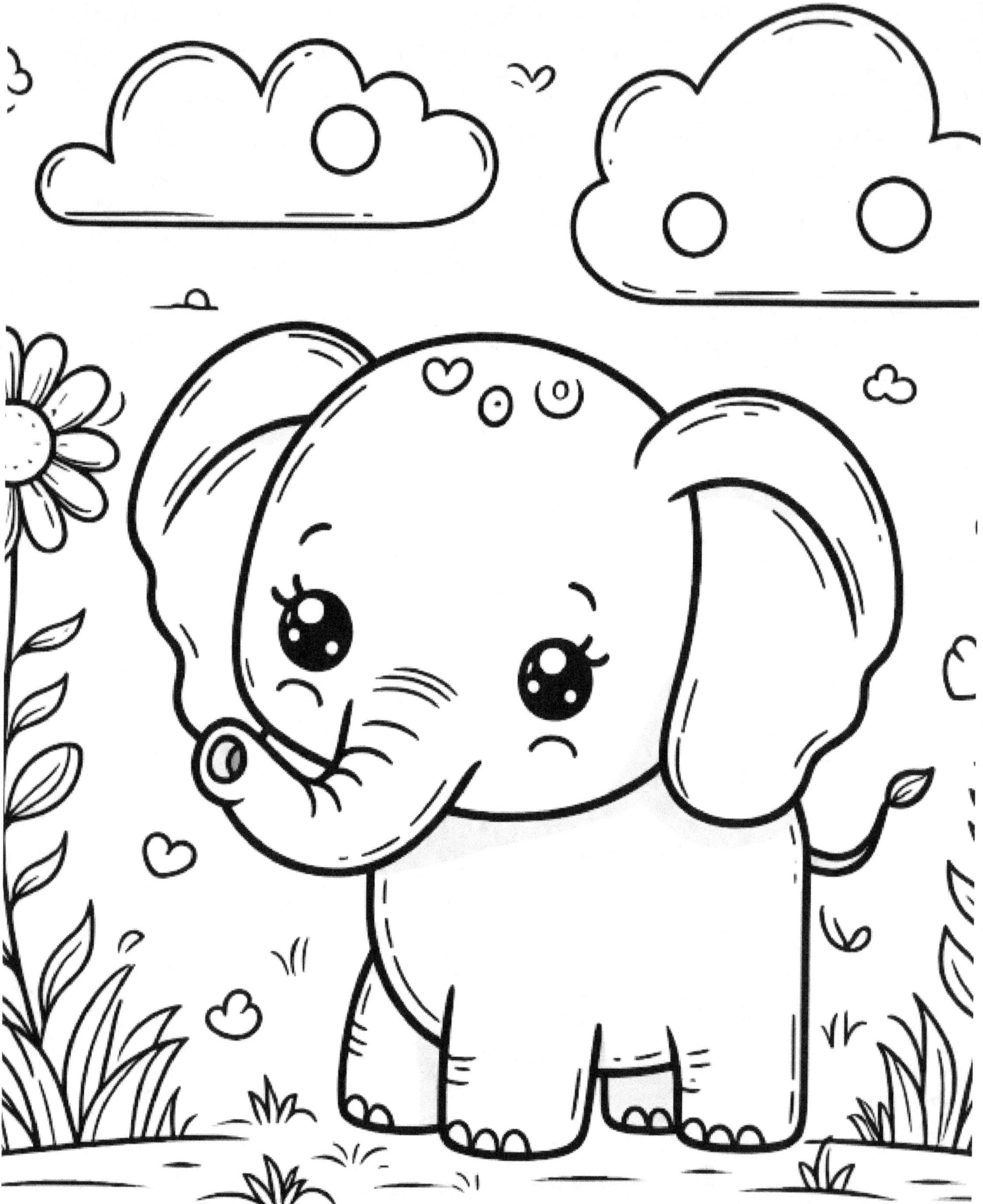

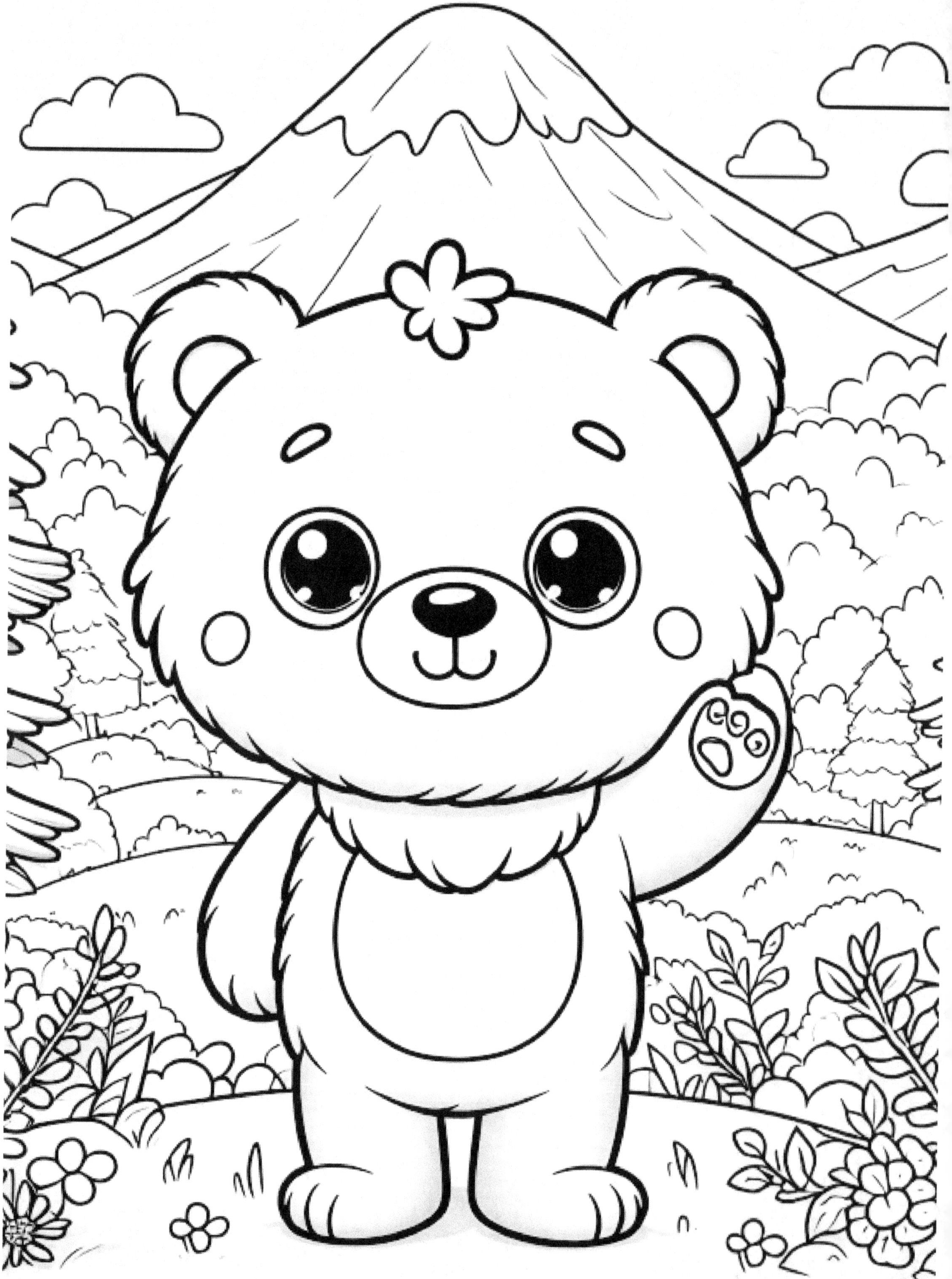

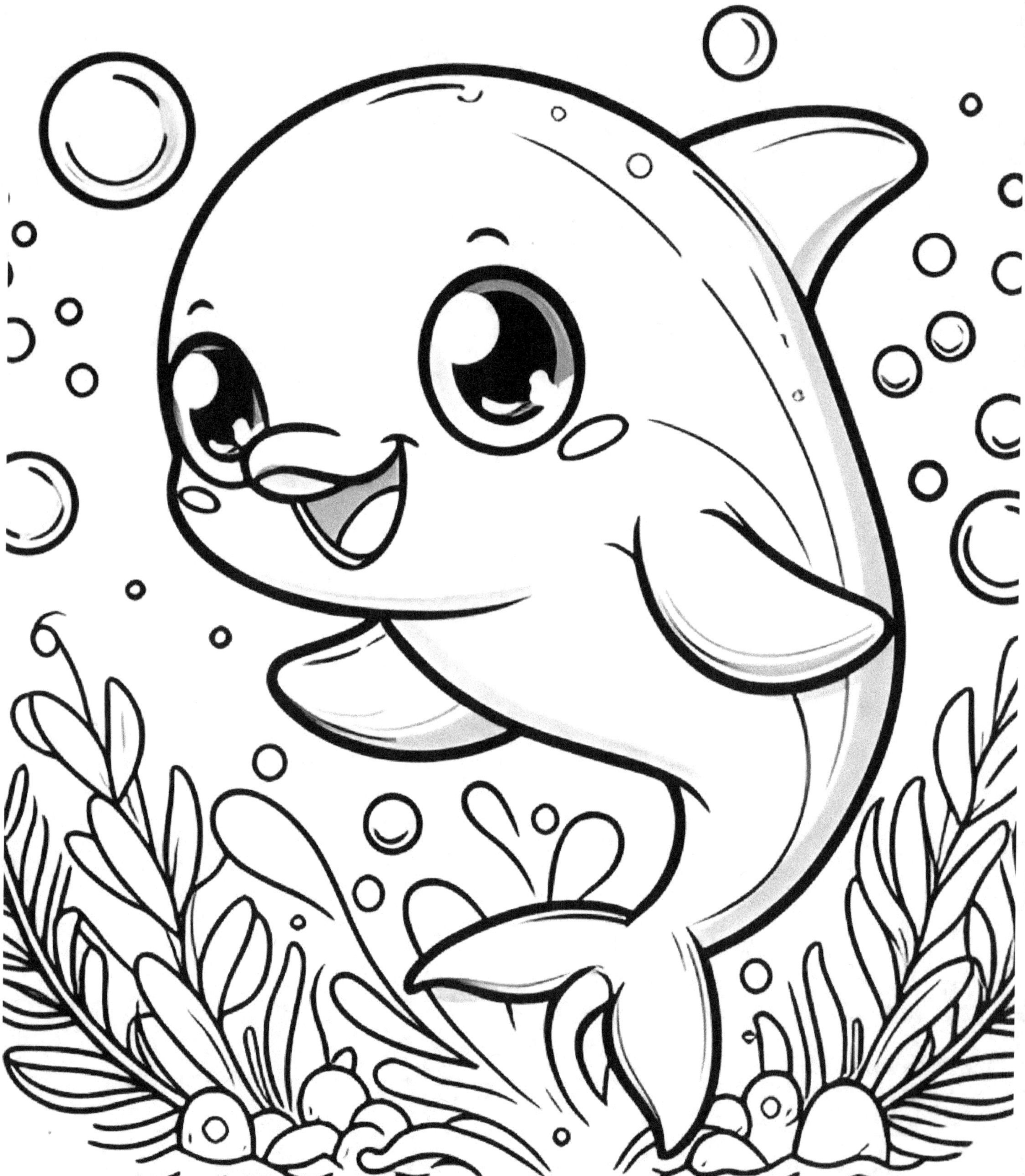

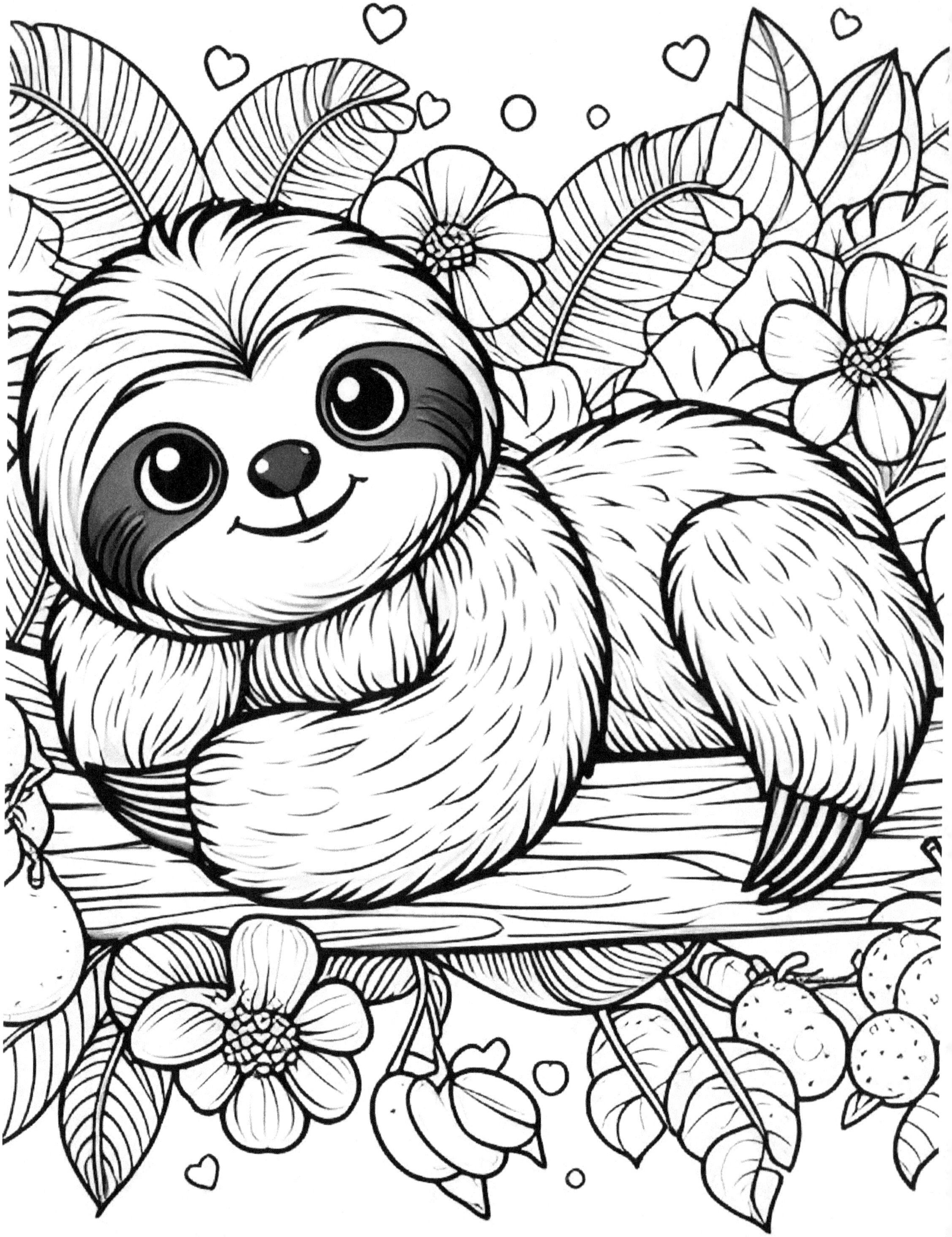

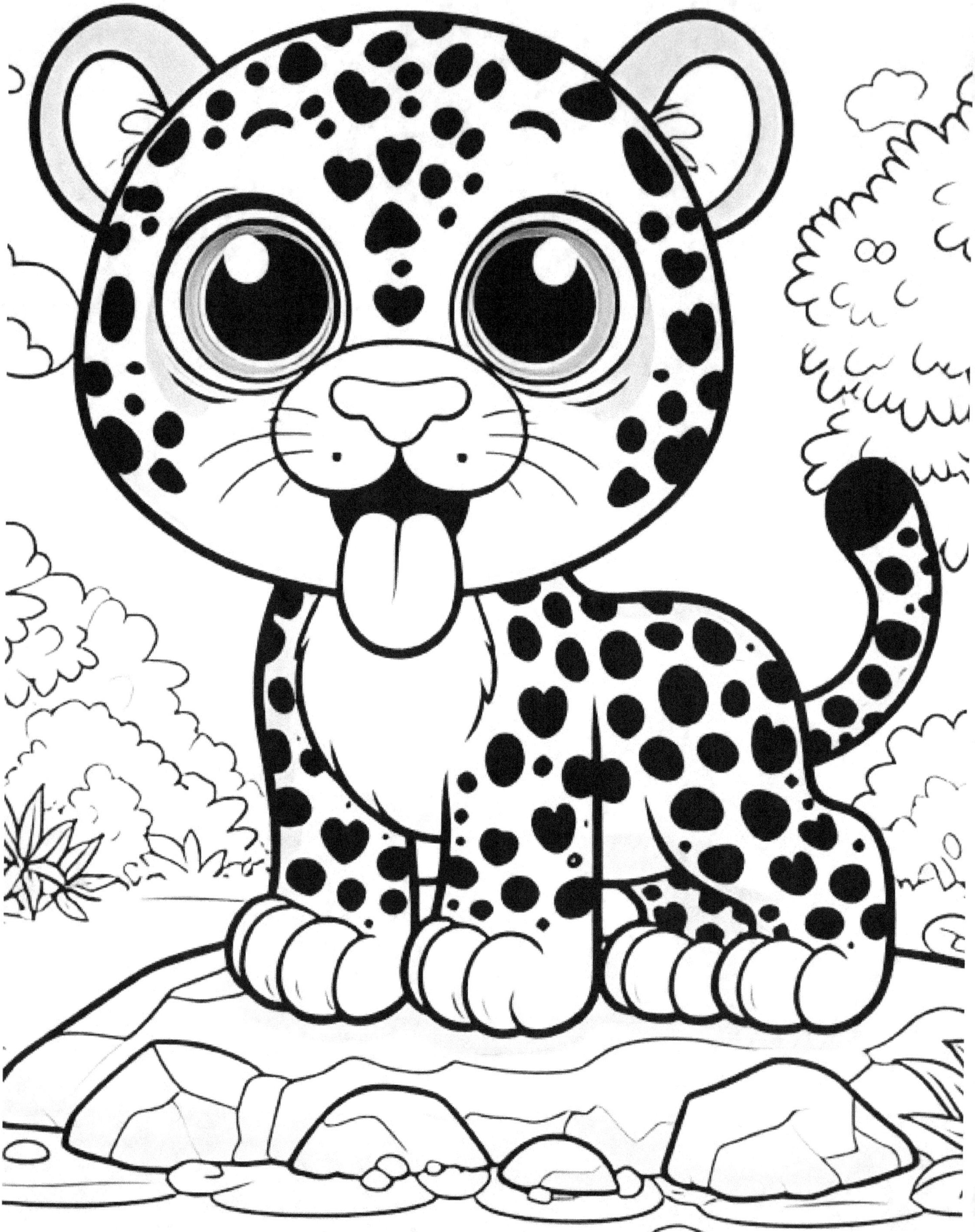

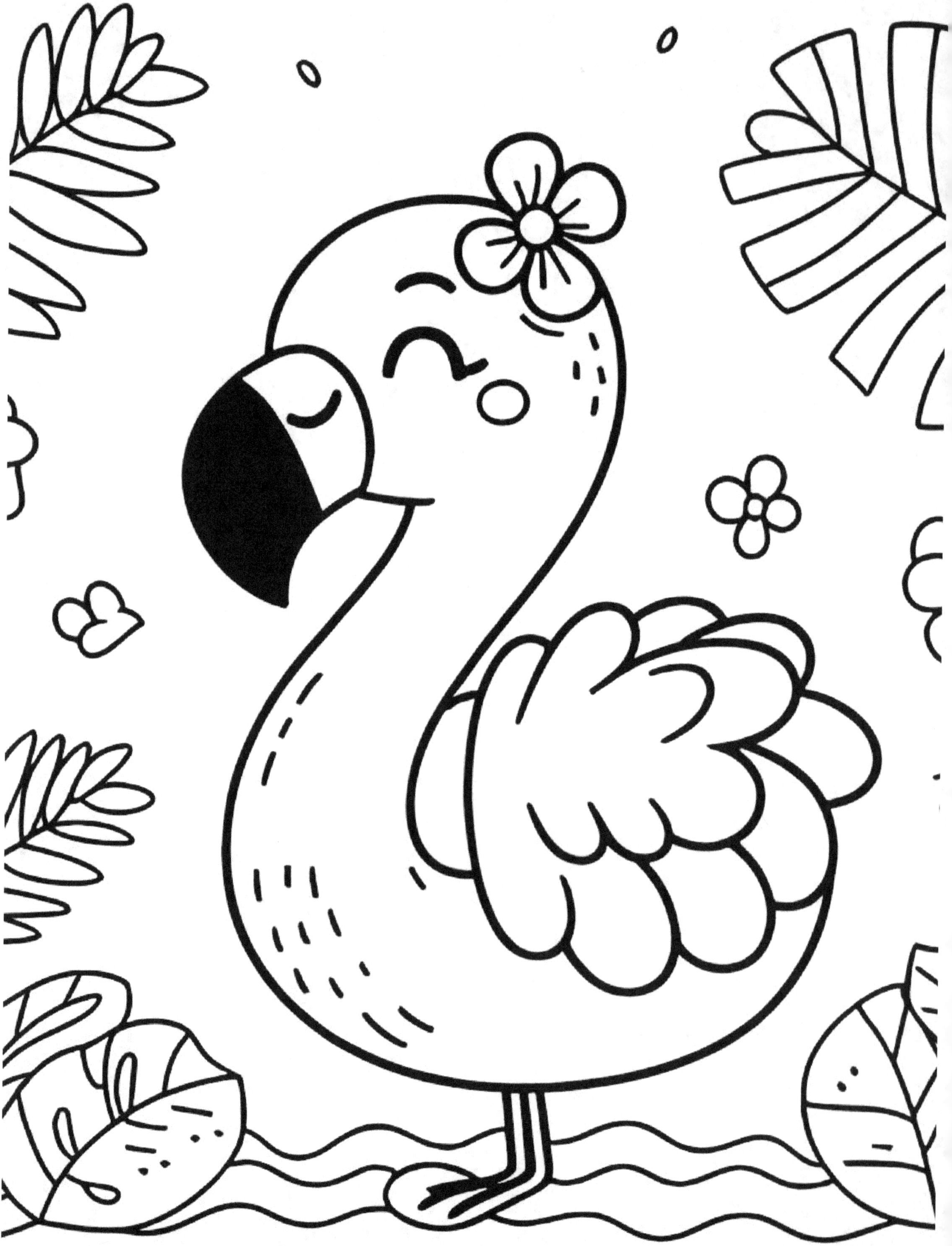

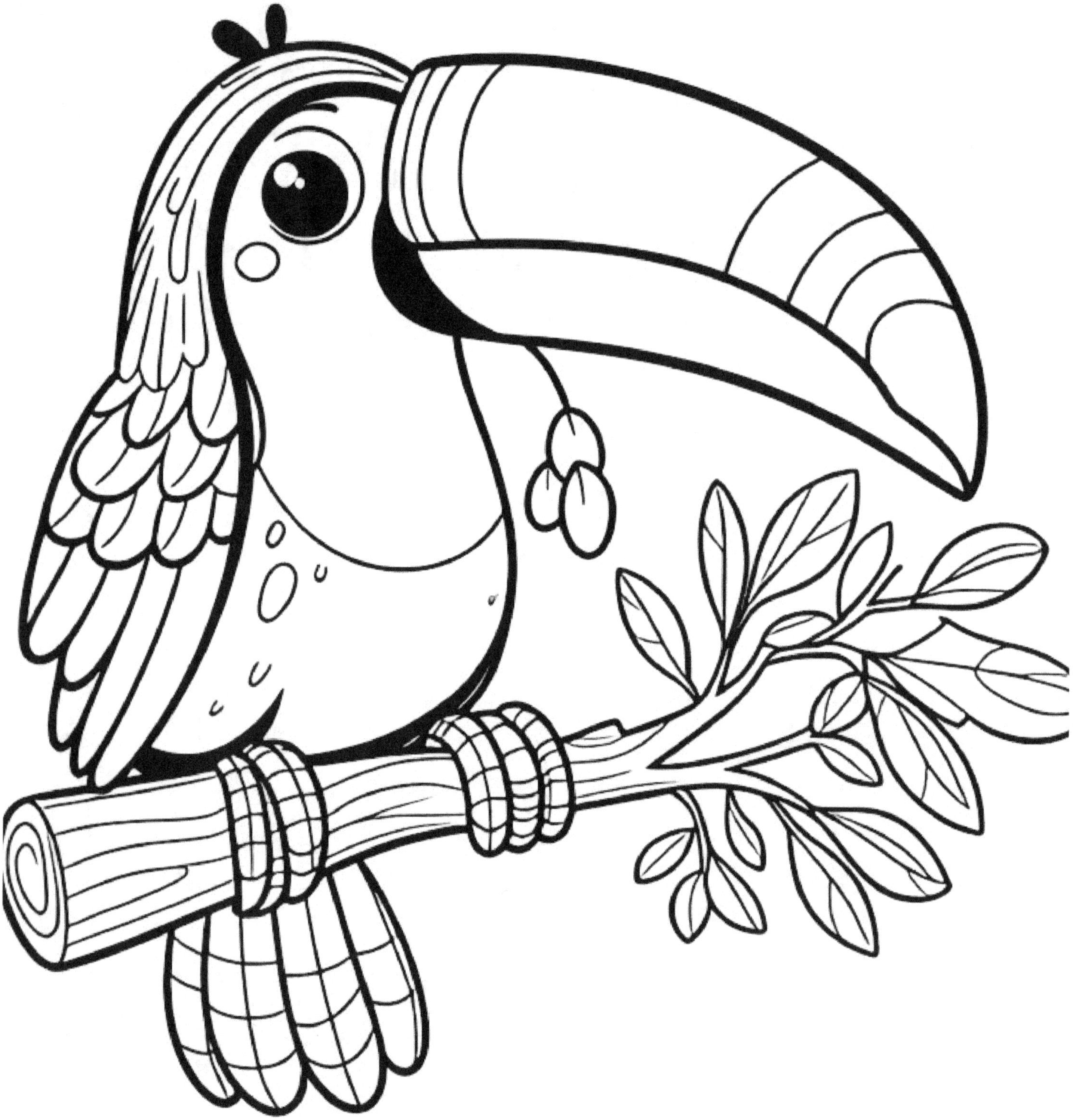

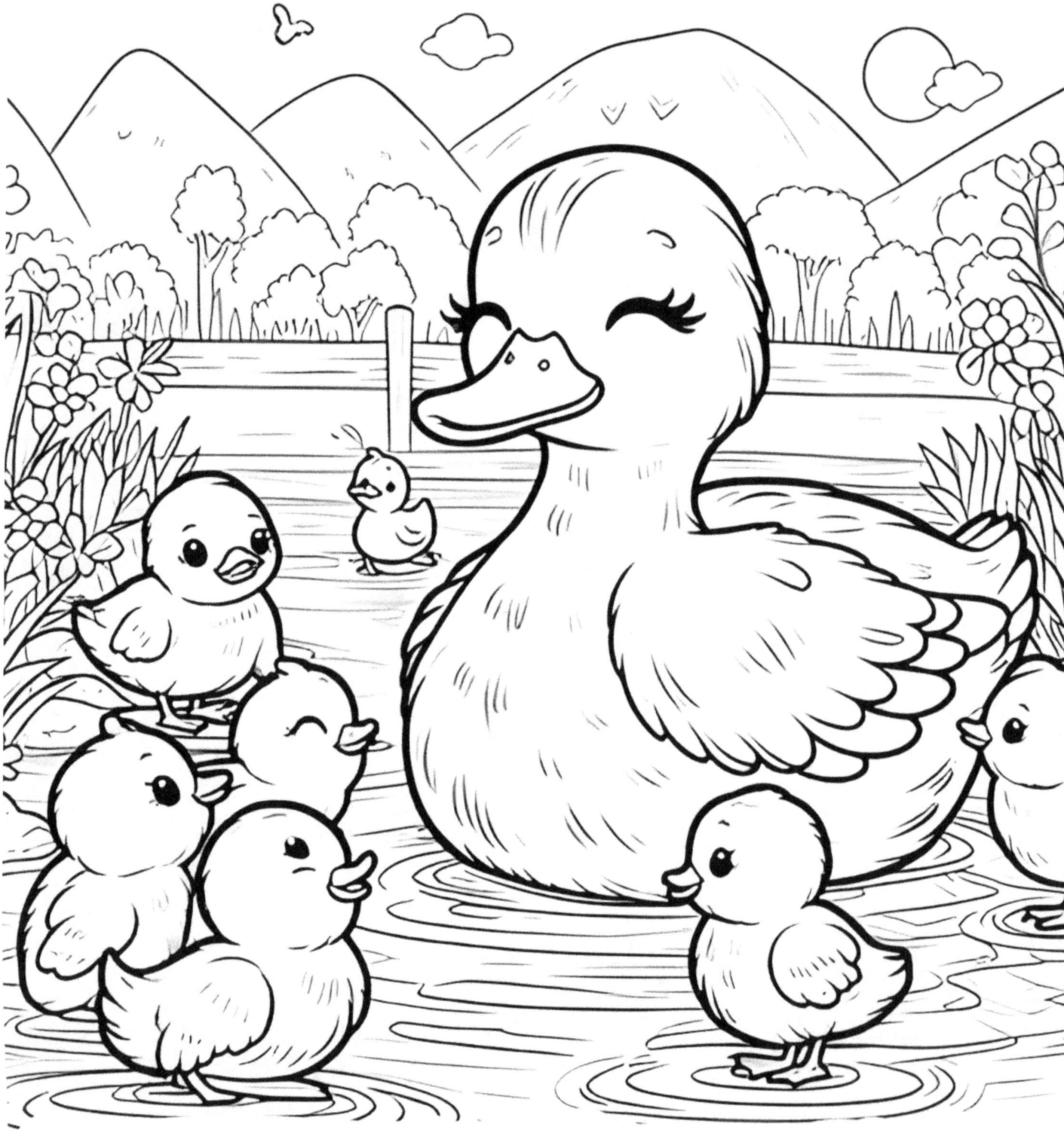

www.ingramcontent.com/pod-product-compliance
Lightning Source LLC
Chambersburg PA
CBHW081000290526
45795CB00009B/3020
* 9 7 9 8 8 7 6 9 0 5 0 4 8 *